Advance Notices for
INSTEAD OF THERAPY

"A compassionate book that sheds needed light on 'inner healing' and how we can learn to change our own attitudes."
>—**Gerald G. Jampolsky, M.D.,**
>co-author of *"Me First" and the Gimme Gimmes* and author of *Love is Letting Go of Fear*

"This is a trail-blazing book that courageously takes on the issue of the therapist-client relationship. It is full of thought-provoking approaches to empowering the client."
>—**Lucia Capacchione, Ph.D.,**
>art therapist and author of *Recovery of Your Inner Child*

"INSTEAD OF THERAPY sweeps away the mystique of the psychiatrist's couch and empowers the consumer of mental health counseling to evaluate and direct the process while it is happening. The book is filled with good ideas, just one of which—the tape recording of sessions for the client's use—can save you the price of the book a great many times over."
>—**George L. Hody, M.D.**

"Lucidly written without excessive jargon, INSTEAD OF THERAPY stands as the defining work on the edge of a powerful new movement. It does more than merely point up the shortcomings of traditional psychotherapy. It also offers a credible clearcut alternative for therapists frustrated by expectations they cannot possibly meet, and for clients who seek respectful, compassionate, and effective help with painful problems."

—**Henry N. Ervin, M.F.C.C.**

"A humanist of the spirit, Tom Rusk has written a book which will return the 'care of souls' to its proper realm, where 'mental' or 'emotional' illness is viewed not as a medical problem, but as the problem of a soul at war with itself. This book urges a return to ethical behavior, to self-respect, and to a 'new' (though historically old) view of the relation between self and spirit, and between guide and client."

—**Charles T. Chamberlain, Ph.D.**
Department of Literature,
University of California, San Diego

Instead of
THERAPY

Instead of THERAPY

HELP YOURSELF CHANGE AND CHANGE THE HELP YOU'RE GETTING

Tom Rusk, m.d.
with D. PATRICK MILLER

Hay House, Inc.
Carson, CA

INSTEAD OF THERAPY
Help Yourself Change and Change the Help You're Getting
by Tom Rusk, M.D.
with D. Patrick Miller

Copyright © 1991 by Tom Rusk, M.D.

The author of this book does not intend to dispense herein any medical or psychiatric advice, nor prescribe the use of any technique as a form of treatment for psychological or medical problems without the advice of a personal physician. The intent of the author is only to offer information to help you in your quest for good health and well-being. In the event you use any of the information in this book for yourself, which is your Constitutional right, the author and the publisher assume no responsibility for your actions.

Library of Congress Catalog Card No. 91-70545

Library of Congress Cataloging-in-Publication Data

Rusk, Tom.
   Instead of therapy : help yourself change and change the help you're getting / by Tom Rusk with D. Patrick Miller.
     p.   cm.
   ISBN 1-56170-021-5 (hardcover) : $20.00. — ISBN 1-56170-022-3 (paperback) : $10.00
   1. Psychotherapy—Popular works. 2. Psychotherapist and patient. 3. Change (Psychology) I. Miller, D. Patric, 1953– II. Title.
RC480.515.R87   1991
616.89'14—dc20   91-70545
                                          CIP

ISBN: 1-56170-021-5 [Hardcover]
ISBN: 1-56170-022-3 [Softcover]

Internal design by John Vannucci
Typesetting by Freedmen's Organization,
Los Angeles, CA 90004

91 92 93 94 95 96 10 9 8 7 6 5 4 3 2 1
First Printing, August 1991

Published and Distributed in the United States by
Hay House, Inc.
P.O. Box 6204
Carson, CA 90749-6204 USA

Printed in the United States of America on Recycled Paper

Dedication

To Judy, Scott, Natalie and Carl for loving me while I struggled to find and accept myself, and for helping me learn to appreciate what's really important.

Acknowledgements

As senior author I have the opportunity and privilege to thank those who have helped to make this book possible. But how can I begin to express my appreciation to my co-author, D. Patrick Miller? Somehow he has taken our conversations and my notes and crafted these chapters, donating his own insights and regularly refining my understanding by his questions. I take full responsibility for the ideas in the book, but he deserves the greatest credit.

Laurie Fox contributed in so many ways. She was the matchmaker—characteristically gracious, giving and wise, she sidestepped my offer and suggested Patrick as a more appropriate co-author. She edited our manuscript, improving it significantly. As assistant to our agent, Linda Chester, Laurie has been our trustworthy and effective liaison with Hay House. I thank her for all this and for our friendship.

My staunchest supporter and invariably optimistic cheerleader, Linda Chester was the driving force behind this project. An author cannot ask for a greater gift than an agent who deeply believes in him and what he has to say.

We owe everyone at Hay House—Louise, Jim Leary, Reid Tracy and our kind editor Dan Olmos— a great debt of gratitude for their patience with us while we struggled to select the title, for their under-standing of our message and for their willingness to risk wholeheartedly backing this controversial book with their time, energy and money.

To M.N., C.D. and D.M. I offer my admiration and appreciation for their generosity, courage and candor. My thanks also to Arthur Weisbach, Don Tonkyro and Carlo Cetti for reviewing portions of the manuscript.

I hope Jan, my right hand for 18 years, knows how impossible it would be without her.

Table of Contents

Preface xiii

PART I: THE FUNDAMENTALS OF CHANGING YOURSELF

Prologue: *The Case of the Miserable Psychiatrist* ...   3

Chapter 1: *Are You Creating Your Life—*
            Or Just Coping? 11

Chapter 2: *What Are Feelings For?* 29

Chapter 3: *Facing the Awkwardness of Change* 59

PART II: FINDING A GUIDE TO HELP YOU CHANGE

Prologue: *The Woman Who Stole to Care* 87

Chapter 4: *The Limitations of Psychotherapy* 95

Chapter 5: *Inside the Guided Self-Change Session* ... 117

Chapter 6: *"Teach Me, Don't Treat Me":*
            Helping Your Therapist Change 145

Chapter 7: *When Is Therapy Appropriate?* 171

PART III: HOW CHANGING YOURSELF WILL CHANGE THE WORLD

Prologue: *Welcome to a World of Change* 195

Chapter 8: *Self-Change and the Human Future* 199

Chapter 9: *Changing Business in Changing Times:
The Ethical Route to Long-Term Profits* 221

Appendix: *Worksheets and Agreements for
Guided Self-Change* 239

Preface

This book presents a new approach to psychological counseling called "guided self-change." This approach is educational rather than medical; it helps people learn to solve their own problems and find the courage to change their lives in practical and meaningful ways.

As a psychiatrist who has stopped practicing psychotherapy in order to be a "coach of change," I think it is time that we stop viewing psychological difficulties as *symptoms* of mental or emotional illness, and begin to see them as *signs of imbalance* between the mental, emotional, physical, and spiritual aspects of a person's life. I believe that the way to correct such imbalances and find the way to one's authentic life is through courageous, responsible acts of self-change.

I've outlined the challenges and difficulties of self-change in my two previous books, *I Want to Change But I Don't Know How* and *Mind Traps*. The first part of this book presents an update on the fundamentals of the self-change process, including the all-important approach to understanding and using feelings to help guide one's life. Part II discusses the problems of psychotherapy and the specific techniques of guided self-change. It also offers explicit advice on how readers can help their therapists become self-change guides. The final section of the book discusses how the self-change philosophy may be applied to issues of social change and spiritual growth; the last chapter focuses on business practices. Such subjects are rarely if ever discussed in books about psychological counseling, but guided self-change helps people make vital connections between their inner growth and the challenges of the world "out there."

□

Although I am a psychiatrist, and therefore a medical doctor, I no longer believe that the language of science or medicine applies to the work that I do with my clients. I'm one of a growing number of psychological counselors who believe that psychological healing did not ever belong in the realm of medicine.

The focus of all counseling is on helping us learn to change our relationships with ourselves and others. I believe this kind of learning is really no different than any other deliberate learning. First, we must be highly motivated and willing to become someone more capable and wise. Then we must study, use others as models, and practice what we are learning. Practice includes enduring the awkwardness of feeling and acting in new and unfamiliar ways. Recognizing this process for what it is makes it clear that personal change—the only real "cure" for most psychological difficulties—is best considered an educational rather than a therapeutic enterprise.

The "mistaken identity" of therapy as a form of medical treatment is a fundamental error that has led to many misuses and abuses of professional caring relationships. Those abuses have, in turn, led to a rising tide of criticism of conventional psychotherapy . The medical model for counseling people with psychological difficulties makes two crucial errors: It identifies the person in need of professional help as ill or defective, and it pays too little attention to the inner, *self-healing* potential of the "patient." I refer to that self-healing potential as the *inner spirit*, the innate part of everyone that instinctively knows the way to health (just like the body's built-in immune system), and has a sense of right and wrong that goes beyond a petty, I-know-better moralism or mere self-protection.

This spiritual "true self" unifies our talents, needs, vulnerabilities, and energy in a way that our egotistic self cannot. It's the real source of our deep compassion, moral greatness, and flashes of brilliance. When someone is said to "rise above" himself or herself, it really means that the daily, egotistic self has been transcended and the person's authentic spirit has come shining through. That's always a healing experience—for oneself and everyone around—and it goes far beyond the "adjustment" to societal norms that psychotherapy has traditionally encouraged.

For many people, modern spirituality seems to be more personal than institutionally religious. The growth of meditation, New Age practices, and Eastern philosophies in the West are among the signs of this development. The philosophy behind guided self-change—for it is a philosophy, and not a science—endorses no particular religious beliefs beyond the idea that an "inner spirit" of humanity exists, in a unique and individualized form within each of us. This spirit needs to be listened to in order to change our lives for the better.

As a physician and Board Certified Psychiatrist, I would be the last person to minimize biological or physiological aspects of psychological functioning. But I believe that the prevailing split between mind and body in psychological practice needs to be replaced with a unified model of mind, body, and spirit. We need not to deny the body, but to reverse the denial of the spirit in the last hundred years by psychologists and psychiatrists bent on the headlong pursuit of scientific credibility. An increasing number of medical doctors in other specialties are contributing to this evolution as well.

☐

Any kind of language both enables and limits our perceptions of the reality around us. Anyone dedicated to human growth and wisdom must be prepared, therefore, to help language evolve and give us a clearer means of picturing our reality. I think it's time that we dispense with "psychotherapy" as the word that describes the professional consultation devoted to psychological healing. I'm nominating "guided self-change" or "self-change consultation" as possible labels for a new process that has the same purpose.

Perhaps someone will come up with a shorter, niftier name for the same process. I'm more committed to the spirit of the change than my present labels for it. To depart from the medical, scientific model of psychological healing, I think we must necessarily depart from medical, scientific-sounding words. Thus, I try to use a minimum of them throughout this book. When appropriate, I will redefine psychoanalytic terminology in everyday language for readers who are interested in decoding their therapists' learned gobbledygook.

I also want to stress that *guided self-change* refers to a process that encompasses much more than "healing words." Unlike most psychotherapists, I believe that the conversations that go on between myself and my clients are much less important than what my clients do *between* our conversations. What I hope they are doing—and what I am striving to help them do—is attempting new attitudes and behaviors, as well as new ways of looking at their experience.

These are the bare bones of guided self-change; the rest of this book fleshes out its figure. To keep the distinction clear between my model for self-change and the medical, psychotherapeutic model, I will be using words like *guide, coach,* and *consultant* to describe the role of the professional in guided self-change. To describe the professional working in the prevailing model, I will use these words:

- *psychiatrist* (an M.D. with training in psychiatry);

- *psychoanalyst* (a psychiatrist or psychology Ph.D. with further training in analytic techniques);

- *psychotherapist* (a psychiatrist, psychiatric social worker, or family and marriage counselor); and

- *therapist* (anyone working in a therapeutic mode).

The word *counselor* may be used for either, but it will be clearly associated with one or the other model by the context. Likewise, I will usually refer to *clients* when talking about those who pursue guided self-change, and *patients* as those who are treated by psychotherapy.

☐

A problem of language that confronts any writer is the use of gender-specific pronouns and adjectives; in the last twenty years many authors have struggled to correct the traditional masculine bias of English usage. To avoid having to write "he or she" and "his or her," my writing collaborator and I have decided simply to alternate gender-specific pronouns and modifiers in a way that seems natural and rhythmic to us. A major exception to our rule will be the consistent usage of masculine words when generally referring to psychotherapists in the third person, because the profession remains patriarchal in attitude even as the number of female therapists increases.

It's important to note that this book was written as an acknowledged collaboration between myself and D. Patrick Miller, a freelance writer who specializes in the "journalism of consciousness." We chose this option over the ghostwriting method because we felt the latter approach would contradict the principles of partnership and self-disclosure that are central to guided self-change. The writing process began with long conversations between myself and Patrick, and this book contains many edited passages of my speech recorded in person or over the phone. We felt that it was important to maintain a simple, conversational tone throughout, and we hope that the book's language fulfills our primary goals of clarity and accessibility.

☐

We live in a time when knowing how to change is an increasingly necessary and valuable skill. It also happens to be the real work of any spiritual path: learning how to grow out of the tiny, limiting self-concept that psychology has always called the "ego" into a sense of self that is much more realistic yet exciting, humble yet expansive—and always in touch with the mysterious spiritual source of all creation.

Thus, this book is for people who are simply too ambitious to put up with therapy. They aren't interested in merely getting "fixed;" they want to go beyond problem-labeling and coping with ego-centered difficulties to contact their unique and authentic potential. And while they recognize the need for informed, caring, and experienced assistance, they know that no one is in a better position than themselves to take charge of their own transformation. I hope this book helps you take charge of your own psychological and spiritual growth, so that you can contribute your caring and creativity to a troubled but lovely world in the midst of great change.

Tom Rusk, M.D.
May 1991

PART I

THE FUNDAMENTALS OF
CHANGING YOURSELF

Part I:
PROLOGUE

The Case of the Miserable Psychiatrist

It certainly looked like I was living the American dream back in the early 70s. A 32-year-old Clinical Associate Professor at the University of California, San Diego, I was being paid a third more salary than my position required, since I had come to the university as the winner of a competition to devise an innovative means of teaching and delivering services at the new Department of Psychiatry. I had won a Teacher of the Year award for two years running. Married for thirteen years, I had a devoted wife, three energetic children under ten years of age, and a swimming pool in my back yard. For a Canadian boy whose childhood aggression and obesity had once earned him a reputation as "that crazy fat kid," I had clearly come a long way.

So why was I often sitting in the bathroom in the middle of the night, pounding on my head to distract myself from my overwhelming feelings of misery, and sobbing silently so as not to wake Judy sleeping in the next room? Why couldn't I endure lying next to her? Why did I sometimes wish I were dead?

The problem didn't seem to have anything to do with work. In fact, I was some kind of a hero there. I thought nothing of putting in eighty or ninety hours a week as professor, psychiatrist, and administrator. I was too busy to be unhappy at the university, and I always looked forward to going home for rest, relaxation, and reunion with my family.

But something always went wrong when I came through the door. Without intending to, I suddenly became sullen, stern, and withdrawn. For a while Judy tried to ask me what was wrong, but she gave up after months of my replying, "Nothing. Just leave me alone." When the kids wanted me to play, I'd tell them to stop being silly. And when everybody started getting sarcastic to provoke me—the kids loved to needle me about being an absent-minded professor, which I was—I began to feel very abused and resentful.

That's how I ended up lying awake at night, trying to make sure my body didn't touch Judy's because that might make her think I felt close. I actually hated her half the time for being happy and close to the kids—and especially for joining in with them to kid me sometimes. I'd think about going to another room to sleep, but I knew Judy would come in and ask me what was wrong. So I began to live my secret life of misery in the bathroom, alternating between weeping in despair and concocting desperate fantasies of how I would, someday, exact my personal justice.

My favorite fantasy had to do with confronting Judy with some piece of incontestable proof of her bad treatment of me. Groveling with guilt, she would then have to beg: "Tom, please forgive me for not admiring, complimenting, and respecting you—my brilliant and strong husband, loving father of our children, outstanding psychiatrist, distinguished professor, innovative administrator, and excellent provider for our family. I'll change my ways completely. I'll treat you with respect and I'll hug and kiss you at every opportunity. I'll make you happy—I promise!''

This was an especially ironic fantasy, because I was in no condition to accept what I really wanted to hear Judy say: that I was a good person who deserved respect and happiness. Although I didn't realize it at the time, I was suffering burn-out from my workaholic attempts to prove myself. I never told anyone how much time I wasted looking around me to find people with whom I could compare myself unfavorably. There was always someone who was smarter, or more accomplished, or more appreciated. Of course, I focused only on people who seemed to have characteristics I envied, who seemed to be what I believed I was not. This was my private, self-flagellating, no-win game—a tortuous game which I had played perpetually since grade school.

No one close to me realized how inadequate and flawed I believed myself to be, although Judy sensed much of my fear about failure—and success. I was embarrassed by what others might think of me if they discovered how frightened, lonely and weak I felt behind my assertive, confident mask. As a result, I couldn't accept compliments that people gave me at work, and I couldn't loosen up enough to be a decent father and husband at home.

In many ways, I owe my escape from this terrible trap to the bathroom mirror. During many silent, miserable moments of staring at my own tear-streaked face in the middle of the night, a crucial question began to piece itself together in my mind: *Did I respect myself as the person I was at home?* I wanted my family's respect and caring, but I knew I wasn't being respectful and caring to them. In the scattered moments of objectivity when I could bear to review my own behavior with my family, I began to realize that they had less and less reason to like me. But I was still mad as hell at them.

Eventually, this anger and my fragments of self-reflection came together to form a decision that would change my life forever. *I was going to begin behaving magnificently at home, treating my family with faultless respect and understanding.* Then, I told myself, if they continued to disrespect me, I'd leave them and find someone to be with who would treat me well, someone with whom I wouldn't have to be miserable and lonely in my own home.

While I was gathering the resolve to implement this decision (and trying to figure out how to be caring and respectful to my family, since I was so long out of practice), something unexpected happened at work that raised other crucial questions in my mind. Two friends came to me, independently, to warn me that they thought I was killing myself at work. "You look pasty," said one; "You're always wired," said another. They both predicted a heart attack for me if I continued on my present track. And in different ways, each of them told me that I was a very special human being with many things to offer people, and that I didn't seem to appreciate my own talents and usefulness.

I silently carried my friends' opinions home with me and into my late-night ruminations. "Oh my

God," I thought while staring into the mirror, "am I really killing myself?" Although I was no longer severely obese, I wasn't exercising or eating well, and I didn't know how to relax. Then an even more troublesome question arose: *What if my friends are right about my talents and usefulness?* That thought really terrified me—which was an amazing thing, I suddenly realized. Why should I be so frightened by the possibility of having something worthwhile to offer?

This was the beginning of my campaign to change myself. Shaken by my friends' positive regard and caring, and determined to give my family no reason to mistreat me any longer, I began to experiment with new ways of behaving. I cut down my work hours, which provoked my boss to remark that he hadn't been able to understand why I was working so much in the first place (he'd been worried about me, too). I demanded responsibility for some of the family meals and carpooling for the kids' trips to school. I made it clear that I wanted to participate in every decision about their schooling, instead of letting Judy decide everything.

Gradually, I began to transform myself from being Judy's sullen oldest child to her responsible adult partner. I became almost fanatic about listening carefully to the kids at dinner, deliberately reaching out to ask them how they were doing. At first, many of these new behaviors felt strange and awkward, although my family took them in stride. Because everyone had seen me go through various kinds of behavioral experiments when I was training to be a psychiatrist, they thought this phase would pass like all the others. But they had no idea of the desperation behind it—I still wasn't sharing that. Asking for or accepting comforting was foreign to me.

Sometimes I had to use my own pride as a tool to pry loose my habitual ways of being. After counseling a couple on better communication one day, I realized that I might be able to practice a little of what I preached. So I drove home and told Judy that I no longer wanted her to tolerate my being sullen and withdrawn. "If I come home some day feeling bad and I won't talk," I told her, "you can tell me to move into a motel until I *will* talk again. That's only fair." More than a little surprised, Judy replied, "You're kidding! You're telling me that you *want* me to say that?" "Right," I said. Then she collected her wits enough to answer, "OK. I'm just a little embarrassed that I didn't think of it myself."

But from that day forward, Judy never had the opportunity to exercise her right of banishment. To avoid being humiliated in such a way, I quickly began learning to tell her when I was feeling bad, even if I couldn't explain exactly what was wrong. And we both soon came to realize that all she needed to do was to be comforting and understanding—not to come up with solutions for any of my problems.

Over the next several years, my life began to be healed. I can't say it was an easy process, but I can definitely say it was worth all the discomfort, awkwardness, and often frightening experimentation I had to go through. I can look back now and see that much of my problem had to do with the unhappy, "crazy fat kid" who was still inside me in my early thirties—but just knowing that wouldn't have provided me with a means for change. Nor did being a successful "mind doctor" do me much good, because there was a huge barrier between the counseling I did for others and my own problems.

Now I realize what courage is, and its relationship to self-respect. Being afraid, as I often am, doesn't mean I'm a coward. As long as I do what I sense is right despite my fears, I am a hero, and deserve my own self-respect. Earning this respect, and opening myself to compassion for my pain, has allowed me to move from self-doubt to a warm and caring self-acceptance. I am no longer trapped on a treadmill of making relentless and futile efforts to prove my worth. Now I have the freedom to use my unique abilities as well as I can in order to discover what I have to offer. I have the freedom to put my efforts, experience, and God-given talents into whatever fulfills me most and gives the greatest benefit to others.

I have come to understand that there is a tremendous resistance to feeling compassion for oneself— and to accepting it from others—when one has not received enough compassion in early childhood. That's a monumental struggle, much harder than extending compassion to someone else in need. To become the *agent* and *object* of your own healing is quite a task—the task I call "self-change." And I now believe that self-change is the only route to psychological healing, because it's the route that restores *respect, understanding, caring,* and *fairness* to people's lives.

These are four fundamental, universal human values that affirm and promote the human spirit in all circumstances. Learning how to revive them in my own life led me out of my misery. Learning how to help others understand and implement them in their own lives is what led to this book.

CHAPTER 1

Are You Creating Your Life— or Just Coping?

And the chief captain answered,
With a great sum obtained I this freedom.
And Paul said, But I was free born.
                                                    —Acts 22:28

Do you feel free? Are you in charge of your decisions and actions—and do you decide and act from a strong sense of inner worth and confidence? Are you free to be truthful with your friends, loved ones, and co-workers? Do you feel that you're in touch with your deep inner spirit, following its lead in creating a unique and purposeful life? Are you free to be true to yourself?

Such questions express the psychological and spiritual search of our time—a time when our ideas about freedom, happiness, and success are rapidly changing. In America, we have a great number of people enjoying political liberties and personal wealth unsurpassed in human history. These conditions are envied and increasingly emulated by the rest of the world. Yet certainly no one would claim that we have discovered the secret to human happiness. We are troubled, addicted, violent, lonely, and afraid.

We may have the wisdom to suspect that none of us will be totally free until everyone is at least liberated from the struggle for survival and from outright oppression. But "saving the world" seems far beyond our capacity—especially when it is all most of us can do just to cope each day with our own *feelings*.

It's one of the fundamental ideas of this book that how we deal with our feelings is the crucial determinant of both our happiness and our freedom—for real happiness arises from the unassailable sense that you are free to create your own life. That feeling may be made more difficult to attain because of one's physical or economic circumstances, but it is neither caused nor ultimately prevented by outside influences. *The feeling of inward freedom is everyone's birthright.*

Being able and willing to make free choices from moment-to-moment means being true to yourself. This premise brings us to the core purpose of this book: to explain how each of us can create a better life once we decide to reconsider what our feelings are saying to us, and how to use this new self-understanding to challenge our lifelong and limiting assumptions about ourselves.

To gain this kind of liberation is not only the challenge of our age, but also the spiritual challenge of humanity since time immemorial. It is the challenge that unites and resolves all others—political, economic, and social—because we cannot share and fearlessly extend freedom to others less fortunate until we truly feel it and use it courageously.

The modern science of psychology began with the study of feelings, but it has always focused on their pathological expression—from the "hysterias" of Sigmund Freud's day to the "neuroses," "psychoses," and "adjustment disorders" of our time. Partly because psychologists and psychiatrists have always struggled to define and maintain their disciplines as sciences—that is, as objective, intellectual, and systematic explorations of natural phenomena —they have tended to treat the subjective and unsystematic realm of feelings with professional disdain and even fear. Yet can anything be a more natural phenomenon than human feelings?

To this day, many traditionally trained psychotherapists regard their patients' strongest feelings as something to be analyzed away, suppressed with self-discipline, or even tranquilized until they subside to manageable levels. (One could guess that what therapists do with their own feelings is not dissimilar.)

I'll have more to say about the purpose of feelings in the following chapter, "What Are Feelings For?" But in brief, I believe that feelings can be pragmatically viewed as messages from your deep "inner self." Accurately deciphered, feelings let you know whether you're on or off the track of the kind of life that's authentic for you—the life in which you can increasingly realize your birthright of inner freedom.

If you're not feeling a profound, overall sense of self-respect and creative excitement about your possibilities, then you're not on the track of your best possible life. You may have more than enough money, the respect of others, a loving family and professional recognition, yet still be struggling to cope with the feeling that life is something that keeps *happening* to you. In contrast, it is possible to feel that you are continuously creating your life from the inside out. This doesn't mean that you can always have the outward circumstances that you prefer—but it does mean that your sense of inward freedom, of being the person you were meant to be, is undiminished by whatever circumstances come your way.

The difference between coping with your own life and creating it is a big one, and to progress from the first condition to the second is a magnificent achievement. This is the creative process that I call *self-change*. If you are interested in self-change, you would probably benefit at some point from a helping relationship, which therapy and counseling are supposed to provide. I'm one of a growing number of therapists who believe that the medical or therapeutic approach to helping, in which "patients" are theoretically "cured" of their psychological ills by mind doctors, is not the best or even a very good way to help people change and realize their potentials. I believe instead that people who have accepted even the smallest degree of responsibility for changing their lives* are primarily in need of *education*—and education is best provided by those who are willing and able to serve as both teachers and models of self-change.

This book will not only help you undertake the journey from "coping to creating," but it will also help you find the most effective form of help. Thus, this book is an introduction to *guided self-change*. If you're already in some form of counseling that's not

---

*For a discussion of therapeutic interventions for people who are temporarily unable to be self-responsible, see Chapter 7, "When is Therapy Appropriate?"

going as well as you'd like, then you may want to share this book with your counselor, and discuss how your helping relationship can be improved. That's not only within your rights as a "consumer" of therapy or counseling, but it's also a step toward making your helping relationship healthier, more realistic, and more efficient. (See Chapter 6, "Teach Me, Don't Treat Me," for details.)

It's very important to remember that we're all equal when it comes to feeling, suffering, and healing. A guide may be a little bit ahead of you in some respects, or have some insights that are new to you; otherwise she would have little value as a guide. But a self-change consultant should regard herself as your peer in the most important respect: You are two people working together to further the liberation of the human personality. Thus, what you accomplish together in your particular helping relationship will benefit not only both of you and the people who are most important to you, but the rest of humankind as well.

Four Essential Values

Unlike the various psychotherapies which falsely claim to be scientific treatment processes free of values and biases, guided self-change is a *value-driven* educational process designed to help people who want to change and grow. I'm convinced that human dignity and well-being rely on four essential and interdependent values: **respect**, **understanding**, **caring** and **fairness**. This conviction emerged from my personal self-change experiences, and my observations of others who have successfully improved their lives. In order to change healthily and grow, we must learn to apply these four values to ourselves and others. This includes learning how to encourage and confidently expect others to extend these values toward us.

Without explicit values to help guide decisions, humans lack meaningful purpose beyond survival at one extreme, and accumulating wealth for its own sake at the other. When individuals and organizations exist merely to survive and succeed in material terms, their functioning ultimately deteriorates into unfulfilling and often unethical, self-centered opportunism. Values are the bonds that allow a life to have coherence, inspiration, balance and generosity. Without values, individuals and organizations lose momentum, morale, integrity—and ultimately their freedom, as financial and political scandals dating from the ''greedy 80s'' have proven.

Of course, values must become more than ideals to be loudly proclaimed or conspicuously displayed on suitably framed wall plaques. For values to be effective they must permeate our lives. When fully in force, each of the four values of guided self-change is simultaneously an *intention*, an *attitude*, and a *feeling*. In the process of self-change, you will find that these three aspects of a value will develop in that order, as a result of your deliberate efforts to incorporate them in your behavior.

For instance, if you have neither much of a *feeling* nor an *attitude* of respect for yourself or others, you can begin to create that value in your life by deliberately *intending* to pursue respect in new, experimental, and courageous behaviors. Next, you must put this intention into practice by deliberately adopting respectful attitudes in your day-to-day relationships with others and requiring the same in return—even if these new attitudes feel strange and artificial at first. (You'll find more about this process in Chapter 3, "Facing the Awkwardness of Change.") Your intention will begin to pay off as your new attitude becomes apparent in your behavior. As respectful *attitudes* become securely rooted with repeated practice, you will increasingly experience respect as a spontaneous and affirmative *feeling* arising from your inner self. As a significant bonus, you will be simultaneously inspiring this feeling of respect in everyone around you.

When we are unhappy with ourselves and our lives, it's worth trying to act in new, constructive, and value-driven ways *before* we invest in therapy. Certainly, a sincere attempt to improve self-esteem and satisfaction by experimenting with ethical behavior should take precedence over the assumption that we are mentally ill, and therefore in need of intensive treatment with drugs or prolonged psychotherapy. Many therapies are nothing more than prolonged, co-dependent collusions between therapists and patients in which the patient trades away personal responsibility for "treatment," and the therapist justifies the patient's abdication of responsibility with diagnostic labels and artificial interactions called therapeutic technique.

If you don't want to consider respect, understanding, caring and fairness as essential, inseparable values underlying our common humanity and the process of personal growth, then read no further. These values are the baggage you have to carry on the journey I call guided self-change. They are also the indispensable tools you will need as you build the bridge from coping with your life to creating it. For the most part, we all have a pretty good idea of what these values mean to us. But many people are not familiar with the idea of using values as *guidelines to the interpretation of feelings*. For an explicit description of the four values from this perspective, see Chapter 2.

Six Transformations

There are countless ways to look at the process of positive change in one's life. You may think of it in terms of sin and redemption, or death and rebirth, or being lost and then finding yourself. The perspective that follows contradicts none of these ideas, while it focuses on the *transformation of feeling states* as you progress from coping to creating. It's important to understand that the negative feeling states associated here with coping do not have to be destroyed or eliminated. In fact, it is more correct to say that the seeds of positive, creative feeling states lie within our unproductive negativity. That may seem impossible to believe before your life experience has begun a positive shift, but it does become clear along the way.

The following table lists six feeling states that are usually part of coping painfully with life, and shows what they become in the transformation to constructive creativity.

COPING	⟶	CREATING
SELF-DOUBT	becomes	SELF-DISCOVERY
SHAME	becomes	SELF-ACCEPTANCE
BOREDOM	becomes	CURIOSITY
RESENTMENT	becomes	RESPONSIBILITY
STAGNATION	becomes	PLAYFULNESS
DESPAIR	becomes	JOY

As each of these transformations is discussed, you can look inside yourself and make your own assessment of how far along you are on the path to creativity and inward freedom. Because we're all in a process of becoming—even when we feel completely stuck—none of us will have a pure, perpetual experience of any of these negative or positive states. But you should be able to get a general idea of which side of the spectrum you mostly experience at the present time. Then you will have a clear idea of which feeling states you'd like to experience less, and what kind of feelings will replace your subsiding negativity.

In a sense, the spectrum of self-change from coping to creating is simply a way to look at what you want and don't want for yourself. Contrast this way of looking at your problems with the therapeutic approach of diagnosing mental or emotional illness and prescribing cures, and then you can decide which method makes more sense to you.

Self-doubt will inevitably arise in a coping life-style. The assumption that we are intrinsically flawed is related to the absence of loving responsibility for our own well-being—because self-doubt is generally a state in which we accept disrespect from others, and from ourselves in the form of negative attitudes and actions. Self-doubt may lead to inactivity, in the forms of procrastination, defensive seclusion, and a reluctance to affirm our unique place in the world. Or it may be expressed more forcefully, when we feel the need to "prove something" to others as a means of justifying our existence.

Chronic self-doubt may also be expressed as a kind of false humility. Rather than risk the discomfort involved in exploring all our potentials, we develop a belief in our limits—and then we may call that attitude "modesty." But we can never really know our limits until we've pursued all our potentials—a lifelong pursuit that leads us from self-doubt to **self-discovery**. This positive feeling state recognizes that our being is essentially mysterious, and therefore we can never know entirely who we are. Thus, we can view our life as a continuous journey into unknown aspects and capacities of our being. Release from the compulsion of *proving our worth* provides us with the energy for the creative adventure of *using ourselves well*.

The feeling state of **shame** combines self-doubt with a generalized sense of guiltiness. It is the feeling of being bad, wrong, inadequate, and less worthy than others, while simultaneously worrying that one is also to blame for this state of being. Physical or emotional abuse in childhood without adequate comforting is the usual source of our adult shame.

Conventional therapeutic wisdom is to get in touch with one's anger about past treatment at the hands of parents or other caretakers, and gradually progress through the stages of grief. In fact, one can leap over the step of anger by seeking out the hurt inner child that hides behind anger. Learning to comfort this child by accepting comfort from others who understand—including a self-change guide who will relate to you as an adult and caring peer rather than an ersatz parental figure—is an important step along the path of turning shame into **self-acceptance**.

The next step is to begin taking consistent, decisive actions on behalf of what feels right inside, despite the risk of failures along the way and the fear of possible criticism, rejection, and loss. To accept oneself is not to deny one's pains and obvious scars, but to bear them with compassion for the self and with the recognition that these wounds are shared, to varying degrees, by everyone in the world. Laying down the burden of private shame makes it easier to lighten the load of others who suffer.

The feeling state of **boredom** may be experienced in various ways and called by different names: *lethargy, listlessness, apathy, indifference, dullness, ennui* or just the frequent *"blahs."* Boredom is a frequent complaint of those who have achieved everything they were "supposed to"—a good education, a secure and financially rewarding occupation, a family and a luxury automobile—but neither feel very good about themselves nor find any particular meaning in their lives. They may even believe that life has no meaning for anyone. But every life has a unique purpose waiting to be discovered and fulfilled.

And whether we intend it or not, every one of us is a model and teacher of what we believe. If most of our teaching is unconscious and accidental, then we are not aware of how we keep reinforcing our habitual, limited sense of ourselves and the world. The secret to escaping boredom is to accept loving responsibility for making the best use of whatever lies within us waiting to be made manifest. When life becomes dull and gray, we have certainly strayed from this responsibility. *Our inner self uses chronic boredom to give us the message that we are aimlessly wandering and hiding from ourselves.*

Yet within boredom lies our suppressed **curiosity**. All of us experience pure curiosity as children, because children are constantly interested in something. Every little facet of the world beckons to them as something worth investigating. Unfortunately, most of us lose much of this curiosity as we move into adulthood, and it's certainly not because we know everything there is to know! To experience the death of curiosity is to lose touch with our inner child. Even infants and young children can lose curiosity if they are emotionally abandoned or abused.

Fortunately, a reunion with the inner child is always possible. As millions of people are discovering with various approaches to "inner child work," deciding to care for this aspect of ourselves and allowing it to "come out and play" gradually restores our natural curiosity and enthusiasm. Those are the energies that lead us back toward the unique meanings of our lives.

Resentment is a festering bitterness about the way things are, an angry feeling state that assumes something or someone else is to blame for our predicament in life. It may be directed toward a boss, a spouse, a friend, or one's parents—or it may even take the form of "global anger," being angry at the world, or mad at God. Minor resentments come and go in the happiest of people, but when this feeling becomes a frequent or perpetual response to the imperfection of the world, it begins to wear down our natural capacity to create the life we want. Thus, resentment creates its own feedback loop. As we spend more time and energy being angry with the state of things, we have less time, attention and energy for constructive pursuits. We achieve less and have more troublesome relationships, and our self-confidence ebbs. Then our anger with the world increases.

But resentment is really just **responsibility** in reverse: The positive energy that gets things done is turned in on itself, in a negative, self-destructive form. The key to transforming this state is to realize that responsibility is, like resentment, a *feeling* about ourselves and our existence. Usually we think of responsibility as an ideal, a moral obligation imposed upon us by culture and society. In fact, *loving responsibility is the natural feeling state of a healthy human being*—one who has faith in her own potentials, and who sees herself as a valuable resource in her family, community, society, and species.

Responsibility implies a certain degree of humility: *"I am not the center of the universe, despite the feeling and the fact that I am the center of my personal world."* This informed humility allows us to deal with the unexpected but inevitable disappointments in life without feeling singled out by misfortune. But true responsibility balances humility with self-respect. In resentment, we merely grumble to ourselves about being unfairly treated; as we grow into the feeling state of responsibility, we can earn self-respect by clearly and effectively communicating that we will not accept disrespect from anyone. Thus, one of the first steps out of chronic resentment is to learn healthy self-assertion.

Stagnation is the general feeling that life has come to a full stop, and that our vital life force is ebbing away. This state of wallowing is often accompanied by depressive, self-destructive and perhaps anti-social attitudes that attempt to justify the condition: *"I'm no good for anything," "It's a cruel world," "I was destined to fail," "Nobody else cares so why should I?"* and so on. Stagnation combines and intensifies the negative states of boredom and self-doubt, and is thus a more serious condition than either one alone. It is also a condition in which the four values of respect, understanding, caring and fairness are virtually absent.

People living stagnant lives may appear to have achieved a sort of peaceful stasis, but their tidy, brittle world is vulnerable to violent disintegration at any moment. The typical profile of apparently "normal" citizens who go on sudden killing sprees, sometimes concluded by suicide, usually reveals a significant degree of stagnation in their lives. It's a law of physics that energy can not be destroyed, and when the natural energy of change and growth is arrested for too long, it will erupt in unpredictable and possibly destructive ways. The feeling that one is wasting away one's life is a warning signal that some kind of effort to change oneself is long overdue.

The key to sweeping away stagnation in life is **playfulness**, an instinctive human capacity that has been painfully repressed in the stagnant lifestyle. Thus, it can require an unusual act of courage to regain the simple, innocent feeling of childlike creativity. It's interesting to note that highly creative artists with strong egos tend to experience periods of stagnant depression just before they begin major projects, and they may even believe that such suffering is necessary to bring forth good work. The Jungian analyst Marie-Louise von Franz has noted, however, that artists can avoid "creative depressions" by deliberately maintaining an element of playfulness in their lives and work.* The same goes for all of us. To play is to release our native spirit from its bondage. *To move from stagnation to playfulness means to risk being humble, flexible, and open to fun.*

Despair is a global feeling that may be simultaneous with stagnation, or that may arise soon after a serious loss or trauma in life. One's healthy sense of purpose and enthusiasm is eclipsed by an overall negativity; everything seems to have come to a "dead end" and there is no reason to go on living.

---

*"*Many creative people start their creativeness with terrific depression. They have such a well-constructed and strong ego consciousness that the unconscious must use very strong means—send them a hellish depression—before they can loosen up enough to let things happen. I have noticed that people who tend to have those creative depressions, if they can anticipate them by playing, need not have the depression, and whenever one can induce a person in such a heavy depression to start playing in some way the state of depression is lifted at once . . .*"

—Marie Louise von Franz,
Creation Myths

In this century, despair was raised to an art form by some existentialist artists and philosophers, and it is still sometimes "fashionable" to feel or express despair about the state of the world. The fact that we generally regard cynicism as a more sophisticated and sensible attitude than innocence suggests the presence of some pessimism and a sense of impending despair in all our hearts. But to maintain a creative innocence while facing the reality of a troubled world actually requires a *greater* sophistication about human nature—and far more courage—because it requires remembering and accepting responsibility for the well-being of our spiritual essence.

If we pay attention to that essence, we rediscover our natural birthright of **joy**. This is one of the most precious feelings we can experience, and in many respects it seems to be the total opposite of despair. Joy tells us that life is constantly renewed at every moment, and that there is every reason to go on living. Properly seen, however, despair is only the corruption of joy, and thus the presence of despair in our lives is not a message to end it all, but to use the energy fueling our despair to begin setting things right again.

First steps may include grieving and seeking comfort for personal loss, or taking constructive political action to reduce the world's incalculable injustices. Like all the other transformations from coping to creating, the journey from despair to joy requires courage—the willingness to fully experience the sometimes excruciating contrasts between the ecstatic peaks and agonizing low points that punctuate every life. So many of us avoid opportunities for rejoicing, especially in terms of intimacy and commitment, because we fear the hurt that will ensue when joy ends. And so we constrict our lives with mediocrity, inadvertently robbing ourselves of peak experiences, and become too familiar with woe. But if we can remember that we would not despair if we did not care, we have already taken the first step of transforming chronic misery into its ecstatic potential.

I want to emphasize that these six transformations of common feeling states represent only one way of looking at the range of human experience. My perspective is based on experience, not psychological theory. I could go on to add countless more feeling states, but these six should help you assess the proportion of "coping" to "creating" in your life at present.

I think we've all had enough experience of merely coping with life to make a summation of that experience unnecessary. We're a little bit less familiar with our creative potential, so here's a thumbnail sketch of that side of the coping-to-creating spectrum:

The creative life accepts one's self-worth as a birthright. One is compassionate and caring to oneself and others, and willing to ask for care and comfort when hurting. Caring and comforting are readily distinguished from mere sympathy or self-pity. Bad feelings are not taken as evidence that one is flawed; rather, all feelings are taken as messages from the inner, spiritual self about what needs to be corrected and balanced in the outer life. The self-creating person is highly motivated, enthusiastic, and curious; there's always a celebratory sense that "there's too much I want to do and too little time to do it in," and thus boredom is simply not possible. Challenges are taken on as a natural part of learning, experimentation, and the fulfill-ment of God-given talents.

Feelings for others—both positive and negative—can be openly and honestly expressed, and the desire to under-stand is consciously nurtured. Because self-worth is a given, all reasonable criticism, even if painful, can be heard and incorporated—while disrespect is recognized and refused.

Creative people are problem-solvers; they are willing to risk making mistakes, and therefore can make timely de-cisions. Finally, the self-accepting person has recognized and accepted his or her inner, spiritual reality as a per-sonal link to the mysterious source of all creativity— whether that source is called God or any of a thousand other names. Knowing that there is no limit to growth— and therefore no demand of perfection—this person goes on learning from failures as well as successes, creating a life as a unique and inspiring celebration of human consciousness.

If you've ever been in conventional therapy, you've probably heard very little about your creative potential—but you've heard a lot about how you might cope a little better with life. If you're in-terested in exploring your potentials, then the rest of this book will help you understand the challenges of creative self-change, and also assist you in seek-ing and recognizing the best kind of professional guide. I've just discussed some of the feeling states that are relevant to the process of guided self-change. In the next chapter you'll find a variety of answers to a crucial question about feelings. It's a question that hardly ever gets asked—much less answered—in the typical therapist's office.

CHAPTER 2:

What Are Feelings For?

Happiness is the consciousness of growth.
—Alexander Lowen, M.D.

It can safely be said that most people never think about what the *purpose* of their feelings may be—or that they serve any purpose whatsoever. Our culture places a very high value on rational thought, and tends to regard feelings as unpredictable, primitive, frivolous, or even dangerous. Despite their undeniable power to affect us profoundly, we generally treat our feelings as lesser or even unnecessary expressions of our consciousness.

We may believe, for instance, that feelings mostly get in the way of our logical plans and decisions. Or we may believe that feelings are okay at home and in intimate relationships, but don't belong in professional environments—an idea often reinforced by the "corporate mentality." (That mentality is breached repeatedly, of course, by emotionally charged decisions punctuating every corporate day. The gyrating reactions of the stock market to certain rumors are assuredly not the product of logical decision-making!) The split between thinking and feeling in our culture has generally given feelings a bad reputation, because it is true that a flood of emotions can jam your circuits and literally make you stupid at intense moments.

That problem is not the fault of feelings, however; it's a lack of coordination of mind and heart. Put another way, it's a misalignment of *personality* and *spirit*. Unlike most psychiatrists, I believe that feelings are messages from our deep inner spirit, the mysterious wellspring of self-awareness that is simultaneously unique to each individual and shared energetically by everyone. Our spirit consists of our talents, our potentials, our instinctive compassion and our neediness—particularly the need to establish intimate and affirmative relationships with others. Our personality is the everyday expression of our spirit, as molded (and distorted) by our culture, upbringing, and environment.

Feelings are bigger and more profound than most of our rational thoughts—in the same way that our mysterious, spiritual essence is infinitely larger than our daily, ordinary personality. Ultimately, however, our thoughts and feelings do not have to be separate or opposing functions. They can blend to give us a vital, unified stream of consciousness. From such a "higher awareness" comes the creative, growth-oriented way of life summarized at the end of the previous chapter.

For most of us, that means letting more of our native spirit—with all of its vulnerabilities and resources—back into our personality. Traditionally, psychotherapy has been concerned only with the health of the thinking, superficial self. Thus, there has been an implicit belief among therapists that life will be better for patients once their feelings are brought firmly "under control." Control is to be achieved by diagnoses of clients' irrational histories, by encouraging their belief in their "pathologies," by demeaning feelings as "inappropriate" or "regressed," and finally, by suppression of feelings with drugs.

In the culture at large, many people manage to keep their feelings under control for decades, through substance abuse, eating disorders, co-dependent relationships, and overwork. But eventually these suppressed emotions erupt in distorted and damaging forms, such as traumatic relationships, catastrophic illness, and abuse of self and others.

The spiritual condition of our society is usually assessed by churchgoing statistics and the popularity of religious beliefs. But I think that our spiritual condition is more truly seen by the way we handle our feelings. The end of the twentieth century has seen a new kind of spiritual renaissance in our society, a rebirth that has less to do with traditional religious forms than the discovery and reclamation of personal spiritual experience. Gradually we are coming to realize that personal spirituality is not an ethereal, otherworldly state of mind, but an all-important means for *unifying our daily experience with our inner awareness.* That means learning to recognize and activate the wholeness of our thoughts and feelings, our beliefs and behaviors, our darkness and light.

I'm interested in the practical applications of a spiritual psychology—a psychology of personal experience expressed in everyday language for the use of people who want to live happier, more fulfilling lives. That's why I'm less interested in discussing the nature or existence of God than the meaning of feelings. Even an atheist could benefit from the process of guided self-change, if willing to consider the possibility that he may not know everything there is to know about his inner self—its vulnerabilities, creativity and potential—and as long as he is willing to examine and learn from his feelings.

The Development of Feelings

If we get our first information about the world around us from physical sensations, then it's safe to say that we get our first information about *who we are* from our feelings. We know instinctively to seek our mother's breast for nurturance—but we have to learn our sense of self-acceptance from the feelings of relationship. If Mother is warm, caring, and delighted that we have arrived, then we will feel good about ourselves well before we have the capacity to think about our worthiness as a human being. If she is cold, afraid, or distracted, we will experience the bad feelings of being ''abandoned,'' ''ashamed,'' and ''unworthy.''

In the first case, our good feelings are telling us that our spirit has found a good home. In the second case, our bad feelings are telling us that the environment is wrong for us. In the highly vulnerable state of childhood, especially while we are still unable to clearly differentiate ourselves from others, it is impossible for us to recognize that we are in a wrong environment. So we decide instead that we are somehow wrong because we feel bad. The fact that our feelings seem to well up from the deepest parts of our being ("in my bones," "a gut feeling," "deep in my heart," etc.) contributes to the difficulty in sorting out *feeling bad* from *being bad*.

Because of the nature of the human brain, our earliest feelings have a powerful effect on our later experience and our grown-up personality. Most current models of the brain suggest that it consists of three major levels of functioning, each representing a stage in our evolutionary growth as a species. The reptilian or visceral brain is in charge of simple, repetitive functions necessary for survival; the paleomammalian brain, or limbic system, carries our emotional energy; and the neocortex, or thinking brain—the most recently developed center of consciousness—carries the capacity to reason, solve problems, and use language. It also enables the crucial and uniquely human function of self-observation—the level of awareness that makes changing ourselves possible.

The great developmental psychologist Jean Piaget's detailed studies of infants and children revealed that years are required to evolve from thinking in terms of concrete relationships, based on immediate feelings and perceptions, to the abstract capacity for manipulating symbols and images. (This is why young children find "peek-a-boo" games so exciting; at the concrete thinking stage, whatever disappears is gone for good, and then it miraculously reappears! Abstraction is the capacity that allows children to realize when something is being hidden from them.) Hence, the young child lives in a world governed primarily by survival functions and here-and-now feelings.

It's also important to note that memory-recording

functions take place in the same location within the brain, the limbic system, that is the physiological seat of our emotions. That's why the memory imprints of the formative years preceding logic and reasoning are exceptionally powerful, and largely determine our sense of identity and degree of self-acceptance. Because of this, merely "thinking it through" is an insufficient remedy for poor self-acceptance as an adult. We may be able to figure out that we are worthy people, and know that we have every right to feel that way, yet not be able to overcome the imprinted childhood feelings of unworthiness.

The widespread recognition of these imprints has led directly to the growth of inner child work, a feeling-based approach to rediscovering and re-experiencing our essential nature, and then developing a compassionate nurturing for the inner child of our past. It's interesting to note that some leaders of this work use the term "real self" interchangeably with "inner child,"* reiterating the idea that we are born with a unique spiritual essence which remains with us for all our lives. The real self retains our native innocence, creativity and sense of wonder. Being exquisitely sensitive, it is often traumatized by early wounds and obscured by the accumulated layers of habitual coping behavior that make up our personalities.

Thus, the messages sent by the real self through

---

*"No matter how distant, evasive, or even alien it may seem to be, we each have a 'Child Within'—the part of us that is ultimately alive, energetic, creative, and fulfilled. This is our Real Self—who we truly are."
—Charles L. Whitfield,
Healing the Child Within

feelings tend to be indirect, garbled, or even contradictory. They are not so much irrational as *pre-rational* messages which one can learn to compassionately analyze and rationally use—or ignore, react to, and act out in irrational and destructive ways. And because feelings are with us long before we learn language, they surface as *nonverbal* experiences that must be interpreted by our rational, more objective selves to be fully understood. (By contrast, thoughts more readily take an immediate verbal form, regardless of whether they are spoken or written down.)

Four principles for understanding feelings are important to keep in mind. These principles can enable you to receive all kinds of feelings with a sense of attentive readiness—rather than a fear of being overwhelmed or a compulsion to control what you experience.

Basic Principles of Feelings

1. *Feelings contain important information, but they should not be trusted implicitly or blindly.*

2. *Feelings speak in a nonverbal code that requires deciphering to be understood.*

3. *While strong feelings are being fully experienced, they tend to interfere with logical reasoning.*

4. *Feelings may feel awful, but they are NEVER ridiculous or wrong, sinful or evil. And they should never be ignored.*

How Values Anchor Feelings

Many people live in a day-to-day chaos of feelings because they do not know what their feelings are for. They confuse feeling good about themselves with the accumulation of pleasures, and they allow the inevitable occurrence of painful experiences to damage their sense of self-worth. If they have been attempting to submerge their feelings for a long time, then some of those feelings may have become transformed into bodily dysfunctions, expressing themselves as chronic illness or an undiagnosable lack of vitality. Pushed and pulled by a never-ending flow of feelings which they will neither accept nor attempt to understand, such people are too busy coping with life to consider that all their feelings need to be—and most assuredly can be—traced to their source in the spirit.

The basic values of respect, understanding, caring and fairness are the spiritual anchors of feelings. Values are conditions necessary for the spirit to thrive in this world. Without them, the spirit is likely to become stifled, distorted, incomprehensible and even dangerous to the physical safety of oneself and others. The solution for a spirit in danger is not its complete suppression, for that is simply impossible: Our spirit is the part of all of us that is eternal, irrepressible, and perpetually creative. The solution for any spirit in distress is to begin receiving its messages with care and respect.

Learning how to do this is neither simple nor automatic. In fact, if we are used to the absence of values in our lives, then instilling them will probably require a period of experimentation that will often be uncomfortable (as well as frequently exhilarating). But to know *why* one is experiencing discomfort is the key to real growth, because a sense of purpose can help us endure the inevitable awkwardness of change.

Following are brief descriptions of the four basic values as they relate to the experience of our feelings. You may want to compare these descriptions to your own current understanding of respect, understanding, caring and fairness. In guided self-change, it's useful to have a *working definition* of these values in mind (and perhaps on paper) all along the way.

Respect is a deep regard for another's inherent worth as a human being. That means appreciating other people's thoughts *and* feelings as being just as real and important to them as your own thoughts and feelings are to you. Everyone you encounter, regardless of their origins, race, gender, class, beliefs or even their crimes, deserves the same basic consideration that you would wish for yourself—since they are, like you, self-aware beings with thoughts and especially feelings.

Why "especially feelings?" Because most of our actions, from the noblest to the most heinous, are motivated primarily by feelings rather than beliefs or rational decisions. (The actions resulting from rational decisions are often soon negated by the actions resulting from feelings, as any dieter or addict well knows!) Finally, it is our awareness that others have feelings similar to ours that really unites us.

Not surprisingly, it is the sense of feeling different from others that makes us feel alienated and alone.

It may seem obvious that respect for another human being begins with respect for humanity itself, but we too often forget this value in the political arena—especially when we decide it is necessary to go to war to defend the particular interests of our nation. Then it is all too easy to resort to "pseudo-speciation" of other peoples—that is, to regard them as "gooks," "dogs," and other kinds of beasts. But to discount anyone's humanity is ultimately to diminish our own.

Extending respect to our enemies can seem very difficult to do, whether the arena is an international dispute, crime on the street, or abuse in the home. But restoring a personal and universal respect for humanity—which must include a deeply-felt regret over our common fallibility—is the only way out. As you begin to experience the truth of this in your own process of self-change, its applicability to larger social situations will become clearer.

Understanding is much more than a rational comprehension of another's ideas. And my definition of this value doesn't imply any agreement with the other person's point of view. Understanding is a full appreciation of *what* another person thinks and feels and *why* he thinks and feels that way. My experience as a therapist, negotiator, and management team builder has convinced me that understanding and agreement are confused in most people's dealings with each other. People are actually capable of understanding each other far more than they want to admit, because they fear that admitting they understand will imply a false agreement or capitulation. Ignoring or arguing with others involves less risk than understanding.

Here's an example: Gayle invites Philip to a social affair that he's reluctant to attend. He understands that the event is important to Gayle, but says he's not sure whether he'll make it. They make no explicit agreement about his letting her know his final decision. Because Philip is uncomfortable about the situation, he doesn't get around to giving Gayle any notice of his ultimate decision not to turn up. After the event, she calls him and says angrily, "Phil, I think you owed me a call. We talked about this last week, and when you decided not to come you should have called."

Philip replies, "But I never said I would come or call." Gayle answers, "That's true, but you knew it was important to me. You owed me a call." Philip, now getting upset and defensive, starts to repeat himself: *"I never said I would call, Gayle!"* Soon a full-blown argument is under way.

What's happening here is that Philip is afraid to admit that he *understands* his friend's point of view. He is capable of appreciating *why* Gayle thought he should call, but he's afraid that if he admits that much, he will be capitulating, admitting that he was wrong and should have called her. Worse still, he fears that being wrong means being bad. What Philip doesn't comprehend—because of his fear— is that Gayle doesn't necessarily want him to capitulate about anything.

If he simply admitted what he was feeling and

thinking—that yes, he could understand what Gayle had expected him to do and he feels badly that she was hurt by his behavior, perhaps also admitting that he doesn't know why he was so uncomfortable and indecisive about attending the affair—then a battle of the wills could have been avoided, and a deeper mutual knowledge reached instead.

Thus, the pursuit of understanding may often require the exercise of courage. Understanding is the willingness to put yourself in another's shoes for the sake of appreciating that person's experience of the world. To do this, you may have to momentarily suspend your own view of the world—and that can be frightening. To admit and work at expanding our *natural capacity for empathy* is the key to developing understanding.

Caring is to feel a positive connection with other people, and a *resonance* with their feelings that doesn't necessarily imply the same feelings on your part at that moment. You feel *with* them, but you don't intervene by feeling *for* them, or by abandoning your own feelings, or glibly proclaiming that you feel exactly as they do. Comforting is part of this definition of caring, without necessarily going so far as caretaking. In fact, caretaking that occurs in the absence of respect or understanding is a symptom of co-dependent relationships, wherein one person actually prevents another's growth by continually doing for others what they are capable of learning to do for themselves, or worse, by encouraging their self-destructive habits. Caretaking can also be a way to control and patronize another:

"Would you like some dessert?"

"No, thank you very much."
"Are you sure you wouldn't like some?"
"No, I'm full. I really couldn't."
"Oh, but it's excellent. You'd really enjoy it. Come on, you'll love it, really!"

In this classic over-mothering scenario, caretaking is proceeding without respect or understanding, and is serving the desires of one person to see herself as a caring person regardless of another's needs or wants.

Another way to grasp the subtlety of caring is by considering what can happen when it is absent from the exercise of other primary values. For instance, a good con man *understands* people thoroughly, but he has no respect or care for them and no concern for fairness. He uses his understanding of people's insecurity, greed, selfishness and self-deception for his own ends.

A clear demonstration of this imbalance can be seen in contemporary scandals involving religious leaders from both traditional and esoteric backgrounds. Because preachers or gurus may be able to speak passionately or eloquently about human nature—and pass on some real wisdom in their sermons or discourses—we may automatically assume that they also care about their followers' welfare. Thus, we are deeply shocked when sexual and financial revelations about some teachers expose their lack of caring. (It's also interesting to note that most of these scandals disclose private behaviors that demonstrate the leaders' lack of self-respect.)

A good way to evaluate the safety and authenticity of a spiritual teacher is to ask yourself, *"Does this person teach others how to care for themselves? Do I feel*

*cared about in a consistent way by this teacher, along with
the insights and instruction offered? And can this teacher
openly admit a need for caring, appropriately accepting
comfort from others when he is hurting?"*

When caring is present, you will feel another's
faith in your inherent strength—and a non-controlling,
non-patronizing, non-manipulative compassion for
the times when your strength fails you.

Fairness means to look upon and treat everyone
equitably, without bias, paying particular attention
to another's feelings as well as one's own. Perhaps
the most common displays of unfairness are bias in
favor of those with whom we feel comfortable—
because they display familiar features in appearance
or attitudes—and bias against those who make us
uncomfortable due to the differences between us.
Fairness means dealing with others based on who
they are and how they behave as unique individuals, instead of relating to them according to generalized preconceptions or stereotypes.

Fairness follows naturally from respect, understanding and caring—one could not conceivably
practice these three values and not also be fair—yet
it deserves to be mentioned on its own, if for no
other reason than its noble history as a spiritually inspired call to political action on behalf of those op-
pressed by prejudice and the abuse of power.
Recent political applications of fairness are evident
in the contexts of "fair employment policies" and
"fair political practices."

Restoring the feeling component to our idea of
fairness helps us see its application on the personal

level of relationships. For instance, many mothers are wonderfully fair to their families while depriving themselves of necessary care and attention. That violates the value of fairness as a whole, and can eventually distort a child's idea of fairness as well.

On the political level, we often think that fairness consists entirely of extending equal material opportunities to all. But when the discussion of fairness excludes feelings—which are often regarded as too irrational and exasperating to be dealt with—then the economic and political arrangements we make run the risk of satisfying no one. *Feelings are facts to the person experiencing them.* That's why the rational distribution of resources and opportunities must always be balanced by a fair witnessing of the feelings of the people involved. Thus, fairness can be a tough and time-consuming job. But it can be somewhat easier when the other three primary values—respect, understanding, and caring—have already been endorsed by everyone involved. Then a bigger and deeper fairness than anyone thought possible may naturally arise.

All of these values are experientially based, which is another way of saying that we know them through our feelings. Part of the human condition is that we can never grasp all of another person's feelings; the assumption that we can is in fact dangerous, because we end up projecting our own feelings onto others and ignoring their reality. So we have to be guided in our personal growth and our relationships by careful consideration of our own feelings and the best information available about the feelings of others. A simple rule for acquiring that information is: *When in doubt, ask.*

When the feelings that we do have become too confusing to sort or communicate, then we can return to the guideline of the four essential values for an assessment of our condition. If we are depressed and beating ourselves up, we may be depriving ourselves of respect and care—in which case we need to risk a caring, self-respecting act. If we are angry with someone's "irrational" behavior, we may be refusing to understand their experience of life—in which case we need to suspend (but *not* deny) our anger and hurt long enough to imagine how the other person feels. And if we are exasperated with the wrongheadedness of a family member or co-worker, we may have to go out on a limb and ask the other person what kind of solution to our disagreement would *feel fair* to him—and then try to arrive at an arrangement that feels fair to both of us. When the feeling side is taken care of, a rational resolution will more easily develop. The secret is to forge an effective working partnership between heart and mind, within ourselves as well as between each other.

How a Guide Can Help You Connect Values and Feelings

There is no precise formula for incorporating values into one's life; it's a highly individual process for which each of us must take ultimate responsibility. However much we might like to, we really cannot give it over entirely to religious authorities, political leaders, or highly paid consultants. But during the process of responsible self-change, we may benefit greatly from the advice, insights, and encouragement of others.

One of the best things a self-change guide can do for you is to point out ways to sort out feelings and relate them to one or more of the four basic values. This can be posed as a "thought experiment." I proposed such a thought experiment to a client of mine, Jack, who was having a difficult time trying to decide whether to sever a troublesome business partnership. He'd been waffling this way and that, endlessly discussing the pros and cons, and finally said he just couldn't get a verdict from his "inner self." All logical and material considerations aside, he just didn't know which way of handling the situation felt best.

So I asked Jack to imagine a future time when his much-beloved son would be Jack's age, and in an identical situation. Jack would be watching the scenario from an omniscient observer's position in heaven. What would he want his son to do, in the interest of his own self-respect?

Immediately Jack replied, "There's no question that I'd want him to get out of the partnership."

"Wait a minute!" I said incredulously. "Are you sure, Jack? In weeks of agonizing over this problem, you haven't had any clarity on this at all."

Jack's reply was certain and succinct. "Well, I'd hate to see my son put up with all this bullshit."

My client's love for his son—which was much greater than any caring he could muster for himself —made the solution to this thought experiment obvious. Jack didn't know what he deserved, or what his rights were as a human being, but he knew his son was a good person deserving respect, care, understanding, and fairness. Jack's inner self had a verdict after all—but only for someone worth caring about. Before the thought experiment, Jack's spiritual "common sense" had been drowned out by the background noise of his habitual bad feelings about himself.

This case reveals an essential fact about the four basic values: They live somewhere within us even when our feelings seem no longer to reflect them. Thus, the decision to restore values to our way of life requires only the willingness to *rediscover* them. Our spirit will respond strongly and positively to their revival, even if they have long been dormant in our lives.

Beliefs, Values, and Feelings

There is a common misunderstanding about the relationship of beliefs, values, and feelings. Despite overwhelming evidence to the contrary in everyone's daily life, the myth persists that our beliefs are primary and control our feelings. In fact, quite the opposite is true: *Feelings are primary and they dominate our mental functioning.* When we proclaim intellectual beliefs that oppose our deeper, feeling-based beliefs, the latter will eventually dominate our behavior.

For instance, the "superstitions" that compete with and sometimes overrule rational decisions in many sophisticated people are generally rooted in primitive spiritual feelings that have not been brought to full awareness and interpreted. When anti-war or pro-life activists resort to bombings and other violent acts, they are motivated by emotions that overwhelm their conscious belief in respect for life. And when free-market capitalists conspire to fix prices or procure special treatment from the government, the culprit is not just "greed" in the usual sense. There are probably feelings of personal deprivation involved, feelings betraying an interior, spiritual void. When anyone betrays their own conscious principles and beliefs, you can be sure that a complex set of feelings—feelings long suppressed and critically distorted—has welled up and taken control of their decisions and behavior.

However, we are so adept at rationalizing our feelings that we can falsely convince ourselves that logical analysis has produced our deepest beliefs. That is precisely why public debates over such issues as abortion, gun control, censorship, and sexual mores become so emotionally charged. The solution is not to force such discussions toward emotionless abstractions. But they could proceed much more responsibly and effectively with consideration of two possibilities: First, that everyone's beliefs are primarily fed by their feelings (including, most likely, some negative feelings about self-worth); and second, that allegiance to the fundamental values of respect, understanding, caring and fairness is more crucial to human welfare than anyone's particular set of political, religious, or cultural beliefs.

It's been said that democracy is impossible without an educated citizenry; I also believe that democracy is impossible without a *self-accepting* citizenry. The only lasting foundation for a fully humane society is the acceptance of values by its individual citizens—not as intellectual beliefs about how the other guy should behave, but as *felt realities* of one's own self-awareness. When respect, understanding, caring, and fairness are accepted and felt as vital internal guidelines, one will instinctively model and teach them to others. Thus, responsible self-change is both a private and political undertaking.

How to Handle Uncomfortable Feelings

Imagine that your whole being is an airliner whose internal guidance system is called "self-respect." Feelings like anger and anxiety are best considered as red warning lights that let you know there's a problem, or serious risk of a problem. If you're a halfway decent pilot, you're not going to ignore that warning light. You're going to check all your systems, in every way that you can. And of course you're going to check that the warning light itself is not malfunctioning.

One has to look for a reason behind all uncomfortable feelings, rather than assuming they are erratic expressions of physiology, "mental illness," or personal defectiveness. Because a greater range of feelings is usually allowed in childhood, we may erroneously conclude that an adult who experiences and expresses feelings freely is not grown-up. But the true measure of maturity is an individual's *understanding, integration*, and *management* of her own feelings—not their frequency or intensity. Everyone

comes by feelings for good reasons, and they are ignored or belittled at great peril. As a friend of mine
used to say, "It doesn't make much sense to keep
your hand on a hot stove and take Valium so you
don't feel so bad."

In guided self-change, I encourage clients to ac-
knowledge their feelings and pursue the messages
they present. The point is not just to ease pain or
anxiety, but to use understanding and caring to
trace feeling signals back to one's own inner sense
of true direction and wisdom.

The absence of positive feelings can be as important as the presence of negative ones. The absence
of great tenderness and warmth in one's life; the absence of caring and comforting for one's hurting inner self; the absence of understanding what one's
life is really meant to serve—all these are serious
problems that can make the experience of life a
pointless drudge.

Guided by the warning signals of boredom, listlessness, and lack of enthusiasm for living, one
could come to the guided self-change consultation
and find immediate assistance for such an existen-
tial problem. A psychoanalyst might well tell you to
sign up for a long-term analysis in order to discover
the childhood origins of your "narcissistic preoccu-
pations." Another therapist with a different orientation might tell you to go on home, because there's
nothing wrong with you that a little vacation or
more fun in your life couldn't fix. Yet another might
put you on medication to eliminate your symptoms.
But I think we should take the signals of our feelings
more seriously than these approaches. To show
respect and caring for the inner true self requires

learning to sort out feelings and understand their messages.

The following three guidelines provide a step-by-step methodology for handling uncomfortable feelings. They also outline the development of "feeling skills" that are essential to the process of guided self-change.

Guidelines for Handling Uncomfortable Feelings

1. *Regard your uncomfortable feelings as coded messages to be deciphered.*

2. *Try to feel compassion for yourself and your pain.*

3. *Do something to improve the situation in which uncomfortable feelings arise.*

---

1. **Regard your uncomfortable feelings as coded messages to be deciphered**. This will require practicing the mental skill of learning to step back from bad feelings to ask, *"What **exactly** am I feeling? Why am I feeling it? What is going on in my life?"* This analysis may involve the use of a journal or tape recorder, or talking with a friend or counselor. It can even be done by standing in front of a mirror, looking yourself in the eye, and literally asking the questions of yourself. By remembering that even the worst feelings are messages from inner spirit about how it is faring today—and not evidence of any permanent defect or shortcoming in yourself—you can eventually learn to examine and understand the

messages carried by your feelings with the precision of a detective. You may rapidly find the reasons behind your hurting at the present moment, or the process of discovery may take a little longer, as you peel off the layers of superficial causes to uncover deeper ones.

In either case, this kind of analysis represents the self-respecting use of logical thought to understand the inner world of feeling. The disrespectful use of logic—which is much more common—occurs in thoughts like, *"It's stupid to be feeling this way," "My feelings make no sense,"* or *"I should be happy now, not sad."* But feelings are never "wrong." They may be paradoxical, and thus they may lead us to unexpected discoveries about our real nature. Or they may lead us to realize that some of our habitual behaviors and attitudes, acquired much earlier in life, have now become unproductive or even destructive to our spirit. Then we can begin the work of changing our attitudes and behaviors—which is the only sure route to feeling better about ourselves.

Analysis of bad feelings doesn't have to be an entirely mental function, however. Some aggressive or highly tense feelings may require immediate expression in a physical form, to temporarily reduce them sufficiently to free up our rational abilities. Much of the violence in our society stems from the acting-out of negative feelings, which violates the values of fairness and respect. To keep the energy of such feelings in line with basic values, it's important to develop a dependable means of physical expression —which can be as simple as pounding pillows or as sophisticated as the study of martial arts.

Some people release their wounded feelings

through violence or illnesses like hypertension because they have no steady outlet for physical energy; in such cases, the spirit trapped in an inactive body is sending messages about the pain it feels. As a self-change guide with a medical degree, I'm convinced that physical vitality is crucial to an individual's health and creativity. But that vitality is better determined by one's own discovery of enjoyable athletic recreation and rewarding routes of self-development than strict adherence to official standards of "physical fitness."

2. **Try to feel compassion for yourself and your pain**. This means deliberately extending understanding to the vulnerable and hurt child within you, who may be responding to current events as a replay of past traumas. It also means stepping back from any self-judgments you may have to begin building a fundamental attitude of *self-acceptance*, which is the only ground from which compassion can flow consistently.

Self-acceptance is not just a matter of public confidence in one's ability or station in life. It is truly measured in private, and truly tested during those "dark nights of the soul" that we all experience. At such times, it can be helpful to think of yourself as another person who means a great deal to you—perhaps a twin, sibling, or child of yours—and imagine how you would take care of someone so close to you who was in pain. By using your imagination in such a way, you may be surprised to find that you do know ways of feeling compassion that could be extended to yourself. For many people, it is an act of genuine and considerable courage to suspend all their self-judgments, even for a moment, and allow the experience of self-caring.

As a self-change consultant, I know from experience that the hardest of the four basic values to practice is care for one's own pain. If you're a sensitive and bright person who has been raised without sufficient caring, then you're generally going to be lousy at accepting care for yourself, simply because it feels awkward and unfamiliar. While negotiating your way through this strangeness, the assistance of a self-change guide who can model and encourage self-care is invaluable. Some people find that contemplating pictures of themselves as children is helpful in visualizing their vulnerable inner child. Others, myself included, have discovered that dolls or stuffed animals serve effectively as tangible, embraceable symbols with which they can identify.

I keep my teddy bear, a gift from one of my sons, in my office. I use it both to comfort myself and to model gentle self-care for men who feel compelled to act big and brave, even when they are alone and in pain. I do everything I can to help people get over their resistance to nurturing the inner child. Doing everything includes discussing my own work in learning self-care, when that seems helpful. Unlike most psychotherapists, I do not turn back clients' inquiries about experiences of mine that may be similar to their own; the practical equality of the guided self-change relationship both allows and requires responsible self-disclosure on the part of the guide. This issue will be discussed in more detail in Chapters 5 and 6.

3. **Do something to improve the situation in which uncomfortable feelings arise**. This means undertaking deliberate experiments to improve your self-respect and get the comfort you require from others in respectful ways. At some moments, you may only need to be held in someone's arms, and will have to experiment with asking for that kind of care. Or perhaps you need to learn how to be candid, fair, and firm with someone who is treating you badly.

A basic experiment that can be tried in almost every situation is to write down how you feel—which by itself can lead to surprising revelations and a greater self-understanding for many people. Or, risk talking to at least one person who is likely to care and understand. That person need not be a professional self-change guide. But a guide may have more objective advice, insight and suggestions for constructive action than a friend, colleague, hairdresser, bartender, or even a conventional therapist—who may not offer more than compassionate listening and an occasional theoretical interpretation of your feelings.

As you will see in Part 2 of this book, guided self-change is *action-oriented*. I do not believe that people must pay for years of expensive analysis and "treatment" before they actually do something to change their lives. In the majority of cases, I believe that people can begin constructive self-change after their very first session with a competent guide. But doing something means taking the risk of trying something new—and facing the awkwardness of acting on one or more of the basic values before they are deeply felt or believed in. This process is the subject of the next chapter, "Facing the Awkwardness of Change."

What Are Good Feelings For?

It may seem unnecessary to talk about how to handle good feelings, because most of us have no problem experiencing them and would like them to arise more frequently in our lives. When you are feeling good, it's both natural and intelligent to "go with the flow." However, it can be useful to analyze good feelings *after* they have dissipated, in order to recognize the context—the social and attitudinal environment—in which those good feelings arose. Developing this kind of hindsight will give you an increasing capacity to re-create positive contexts, instead of mourning good feelings as an infrequent, mysterious visitation over which you have no control. For example, seemingly miraculous moments of deep, caring intimacy can follow a lot of hard work at communication or sharing—although this reward may not be so immediate as to be readily recognized unless one has developed some of the skills of introspection and hindsight.

It's also important to distinguish the good feeling that arises from creating harmony between one's spirit and personality from shallower, pleasurable moods and sensations. Many people equate physical pleasures and egotistic thrills with feeling good about themselves and others, and thus devote their lives to stringing together as many of these experiences as possible. But as many spiritual traditions teach, the sensations of pain and pleasure are inextricably linked. No human being can have one without the other, and life on earth is an experience of their alternation. A life guided merely by attempts to seek pleasure and avoid pain is generally a chaotic existence, in which one lives alienated from self and others.

To feel good about oneself, however, requires the ability to learn from both pain and pleasure, accepting them as natural and inevitable experiences—and as crucial messages from the inner self. If you feel securely anchored in your spiritual self, then it will not be necessary either to become absorbed in your painful and pleasurable experiences, nor detach yourself from them. (In fact, it is only a total identification with strong feelings of any sort that seems to make detachment necessary.)

True happiness is the capacity to be at peace even when you're unhappy, and to know that you're growing even in the midst of the deepest suffering. This means that we can develop a deep, abiding, peaceful joy which is strong enough to weather all the inevitable storms of life; this has been called the "peace which passeth understanding." This is a spiritual attainment which is beyond the ken of conventional psychotherapy, but it is a practical goal for the process of guided self-change—if sought with determination and courage.

In our society, people often believe that they will only feel good about themselves in a deep and lasting way when they finally "succeed" in material or professional terms. But as my own case history preceding this part of the book demonstrates, you can have more than you dreamed possible in terms of wealth, status, and achievement, and still live with feelings of isolation, shame and unworthiness.

Ultimately, feeling good about yourself depends on activating the values of respect, understanding, caring and fairness in your life. If you are a respectful and caring person, you're going to have a hard time feeling bad about yourself no matter what happens to you. If you are consistently fair and understanding to others, you will develop an inner strength and resiliency that can withstand the worst of what others may do to you.

When clients ask me for advice on important decisions in their lives, I usually ask them to consider what option they can choose that will make them feel proud of themselves *regardless* of whether that option proves successful. Often that requires imagining a long-term perspective: If you're faced with a tough decision that seems to pit your values against your desires for immediate success, which of your options is most likely to make you proud to look back on at the end of your life? Can you factor in the spiritual "bottom line" along with the more conventional, material one? (It's true that there is not a lot of support for such value-driven decision-making in our society, but I think that is beginning to change. We've had a television show entitled "Lifestyles of the Rich and Famous" for quite a while now; perhaps we will soon see one called "Lifestyles of the Respectful and Fair.")

Here's another question that examines values: *Would you feel better about yourself for winning a lottery or regularly volunteering at a soup kitchen?* The first may have a very pleasant druglike effect, altering your mood substantially but temporarily; the other could provide a lasting affirmation of your compassionate spirit, especially if the work proves difficult. Success without self-acceptance is empty. Acquiring what you want in the short term will always lead to disillusionment, unless you live in accordance with the fundamental values of the human spirit.

As you change your life to activate the values of respect, understanding, caring, and fairness, and bring your spirit into the ordinary, daily world, the feelings you have will become increasingly reliable messages about how to chart the course of your growth. That is indeed what feelings are for.

CHAPTER 3:

Facing the Awkwardness of Change

Courage is the price that Life exacts for granting peace.
—Amelia Earhart

Clearly we can decide to change ourselves by learning something new. We can become "computer literate," or learn how to play a musical instrument, or become a novelist. Some undertakings are more difficult than others, and each of us has more or less native talent for the particular skills necessary. But given sufficient motivation, we can tap into our inherent abilities, and develop new skills, in order to change ourselves into someone different and more competent. Any one of countless possible additions to our knowledge and knowhow will modify our lifestyle, our self-image, and our identity in the eyes of others.

These kinds of change are challenging enough. More challenging is any deliberate shift in our *fundamental* sense of self—which includes feelings about our intrinsic worth, our estimates of our inherent potentials, and our ideas about our destiny, meaning, and purpose. If we reflect on these fundamentals of the self at all (and many people do not), we may conclude that they are genetically imprinted, or fixed in place by certain significant events in our lives. It's safe to say that most adults regard their own personalities as unchangeable, even if they have grown to dislike themselves intensely. Such unhappy beings must settle for putting up with their own personalities—and use intimidation or make self-demeaning deals to get other people to tolerate their negative ways of being.

In this coping state, described in detail in Chapter 1, an individual will live perpetually with a variety of bad feelings that reinforce his negative self-concept. He may fervently wish that his life would change, but he can imagine that happening only if the people around him change, or if some powerful person, group, or psychological technique manages to change him. If nothing outside himself seems likely to give, then a worsening spiral of despair can lead all the way to suicide. Most people who are coping with their lives, however, learn to tolerate various degrees of unhappiness and self-hatred. They stay alive, but they go through life with bitterness, a persistent sense of dissatisfaction, and regret over missed opportunities.

As suggested in Chapter 2, the first step out of a coping lifestyle is to experience our own feelings in a new way. Whether good or bad, feelings are not *evidence* of our permanent condition, but *messages* from our deep inner spirit about our well-being at a particular moment in time. These messages are not always clear and straightforward, and often require careful decoding before they can be constructively acted upon. The fundamental values of respect, understanding, caring, and fairness are the best guidelines for the interpretation of feelings, for they anchor us in our deepest personal truths, our spiritual reality. Knowing that a creative and inspired lifestyle will naturally demonstrate these values, we can begin to use our feelings as indicators of the kinds of change we need to make in our lives.

This understanding of feelings is crucial because of the fact that deliberate, substantial change in our sense of self is quite difficult. There's no way to go about it without experiencing feelings of awkwardness and disorientation. If we avoid or retreat from such feelings instead of interpreting them in a useful manner, then we won't get anywhere with attempts at self-change. With strong values in place or developing, we can use feelings of awkwardness as signals to guide ourselves forward into change, instead of holding back from it. When we can look straight into our fears and find at least a little willingness to do what we believe is right and worthwhile—regardless of how difficult or frightening it appears to do so—then we have discovered *courage*. This discovery is available to everyone, because anyone who can be afraid can be courageous. Indeed, the absence of fear makes courage impossible. The seeds of change lie within our fears.

The Familiarity Principle

Resistance to change is the most powerful force in human psychology, whether that change be in ourselves as individuals, or gathered together in families or organizations. Anyone who decides to face their own resistance in a courageous act of self-change will soon experience the truth of what I call the Familiarity Principle:

You cannot act or be treated in ways that are different from those you are used to—even if those ways are better—without becoming increasingly uncomfortable.

The Familiarity Principle operates so powerfully and relentlessly that we find ourselves highly resistant to deliberate change even when we are strongly motivated—to lose weight, to be more assertive, to learn a foreign language, to be more patient with our children. And it can operate in surprising, paradoxical ways, as in the not uncommon cases of people who find themselves unhappy and disoriented when their alcoholic spouses finally do what everyone's wanted them to do for years—stop drinking. Suddenly freed of their roles as co-dependent caretakers, the partners of recovering alcoholics may find their own sense of identity and purpose shaken by an otherwise positive turn of events. They may even become frightened and angry that they, too, must change in order to become part of the new life undertaken by their partners.

Where does this tremendous resistance to change in humans come from? The sources are many and complex, but they can be traced to such fundamental principles as the law of inertia: *A body at rest will resist being set in motion, and a body in motion will resist any change of speed or direction of its motion.* Likewise, the health of living organisms generally depends on their *homeostasis*, the state of equilibrium that tends to resist change. And from the very beginning of our life as human beings, we learn that familiarity usually equals safety, in terms of our physical and social environment.

However, the natural processes of growth thrust us into thrilling and terrifying realms of change, both physically and psychologically. Children must become adolescents, and adolescents must become self-sufficient adults. This process of maturing is common to virtually all living things, but the human animal is unique for its capacity to continue changing inwardly—and to *choose* to change—throughout its lifespan. Our capacity to learn serves more than our survival, and we don't ever have to stop learning. In the most basic terms, learning is really the spiritual purpose of our lives.

Although our early learning may chiefly serve our needs as individuals or families, the opportunity for further, mature learning exists and is often wasted. Mature learning leads us toward increasingly inter-dependent and altruistic perceptions and decisions. Gradually we come to see that the highest potential of the human animal is not survival, but service. We also learn that our personal calling into service—whether that be as an artist, minister, politician, self-change guide, or bus driver—is also our calling toward the highest quality life, one with happiness, peace and genuine fulfillment. But at every step of the way, we will encounter our own resistance: the longing to stay safe, secure, and unchanged.

Were we purely spiritual, nonphysical beings, we might have no need of learning and changing, and thus we wouldn't have to face death, discomfort, or making courageous decisions. But the human condition is that of a mortal animal becoming ever more self-aware—recognizing and striving to manifest its spirit in the world. The higher reaches of that process are unknown to most of us. What is within our daily grasp is the kind of learning I am calling self-change.

Seven Steps to Self-Change

Dissatisfaction with life can provide the motivation for changing oneself, but it cannot organize and direct the process. While each person who searches for personal growth will discover a highly individualistic path of self-change, it helps to have a reliable, tested approach at the beginning of the journey. Beginning only with your dissatisfaction about some aspect of your experience, you can use the following seven steps to pursue any kind of change within yourself. Some of these steps are purely mental or imaginative exercises; others require decisive action in your social environment. They can all be undertaken without the assistance of a self-change guide, although professional or peer counseling can be especially helpful at steps 3, 4, and 5.

The Seven Steps to Self-Change

1. *Consider the possibility that you can adopt novel and temporarily artificial attitudes and ways of being.*

2. *Consider the possibility that you can become someone you respect more, someone who deserves more of your compassion and care.*

3. *Identify some particular attitude and action experiments that might make you feel more caring, self-respecting, and satisfied.*

4. *Rehearse your experiments in your mind, in a journal, on tape, or with supportive friends or a self-change guide.*

5. *Use your courage to implement your rehearsed experiment in attitude or behavior.*

6. *Commit yourself to repeated practice of new attitudes and actions.*

7. *Rejoice and reward yourself each time you have been courageous and completed a self-change experiment—regardless of its success or failure.*

1. **Consider the possibility that you can adopt novel and temporarily artificial attitudes and ways of being.** Many people obstruct their own self-change simply by not imagining that they could act or think in a significantly different way than they are used to. They establish a limited repertoire of behaviors and attitudes that feels comfortable and

familiar, and then their personalities are "set for life." The idea that one's personality can be enlarged or deepened by trying on a new and temporarily artificial attitude or behavior—even for a good reason—may strike them as absurd or dishonest.

Let's say that you have a superior at work who consistently acts in immature and spiteful ways. You were warned about him by your colleagues from the first day on the job, and so far he hasn't done anything to disprove his negative reputation. There's a general agreement that this disagreeable fellow simply doesn't deserve anyone's respect, and so you've gotten in the habit of treating him as disdainfully as possible, within the confines of holding onto your job. Like everyone else, you indulge in cutting remarks about him behind his back, while treating him with a false politeness face-to-face.

One day you realize that your own behavior toward your boss has become as immature as his own—and that to continue to treat him disrespectfully behind his back will only damage your own sense of self-worth. To change the situation, you must consider the possibility of treating your superior well—even though he doesn't "deserve" it, and even though you still dislike him. This means that treating him with respect will at first feel *artificial* and very awkward to you.

The difference between this artificiality and the false politeness you have expressed before lies in the deliberate application of basic values to the situation. Not only are you extending *respect* in affirmation of your own self-respect, you are also opening the door to *understanding* of another person's experience. (You might be shocked to learn what insecurity and suffering lies behind your superior's poor behavior!) You do this because you *care* about creating a better working situation for yourself and everyone around you, and because you realize that it is only *fair* to treat everyone with openness and decency. Besides, your respect, understanding, caring and fairness earns you the right to gently confront your superior with your complaint about the unfairness (as you see it) of his attitudes toward you and others.

By considering the possibility of acting in a novel and artificial but value-driven way, you will already be introducing change into the situation. This certainly doesn't guarantee that your boss will eventually become a lovable human being—it may lead instead to the realization that your work environment is intolerable to you. Regardless of your subsequent decisions, the adoption of new, value-driven attitudes and behaviors means that you have already begun changing yourself in the positive direction of Step 2:

2. **Consider the possibility that you can become someone you respect more, someone who deserves more of your compassion and care.** It's not uncommon for people to attempt a more caring way of life and leave themselves out of the equation. People who are trying to escape feelings of self-hatred may end up in caretaking professions such as medicine, the ministry, or therapy. Such people can do good work—though probably never achieving their full potential—while suffering quietly all throughout

their lives. Or they may perpetrate some kind of abuse on others, as their inner pain contaminates their social goodwill.

Thus, this step into positive self-change clearly differentiates the process from that of simply becoming a "do-gooder." To take on a value-driven way of life means applying it to oneself as much as to others, and recognizing that there need be no conflict in the process. Respect, understanding, caring and fairness are not finite qualities that must be taken from one person to be given to another; rather, they are creative potentials within everyone that can always be renewed and extended.

An excellent way to undertake this step is through the use of the "Mirror Exercise." Simply stand in front of a mirror and look into your own eyes for a minute or two. If you can manage a long, quiet look and feel a sense of support and caring for yourself, then you are already doing well in terms of self-acceptance. If looking at yourself either feels silly or creates a distant, critical coldness, then you probably need to face and examine your self-doubt—which simply requires continuing to look in the mirror despite your discomfort. Can you recognize how hard you are on yourself, how little compassion you have for your own fears and pain? After this experience, you may want to record your thoughts and feelings in a journal, and question yourself about what changes you might attempt that would make facing yourself a more positive experience.

I recommend daily practice of the Mirror Exercise to many of my clients, as a regular means of checking in on feelings and the progress of self-change work. For those who think it sounds awkward, I point out the fact that we naturally look into the eyes of friends to see how they are really feeling, to verify or look beyond what they may report to us. If a friend seemed tense or depressed, we would care and try to be supportive and understanding. To begin the process of meaningful change, we must be willing to accept the temporary awkwardness of becoming a warm, caring friend to the vulnerable, needy parts of ourselves.

3. **Identify some particular attitude and action experiments that might make you feel more caring, self-respecting, and satisfied.** This step is similar to the first, but it carries the process into specific ideas for new ways of thinking and behaving. At this stage , it's best to use your imagination as freely as possible, coming up with as many possibilities for experimentation as you can, covering the spectrum from the most cautious to the most ambitious. Then, with the help of a counselor or your own journal, you can thoroughly explore the apparent risks and benefits of each experiment, giving priority to those that seem worth the risks.

Vivian was a 35-year-old client of mine who wanted to improve her problematic relationship with her mother, with whom she was rarely communicating when our self-change consultations began. Fiercely independent and resentful of her mother's controlling behavior, Vivian had opted for silence and avoidance in relations with her mother, but she knew that this solution hurt her mother as well as her sisters; they felt that Vivian unfairly expected them to act as her liaison for home communications. She also realized that her behavior toward her mother was stunting her own growth, and wasting the last years available for understanding her surviving parent and her own childhood.

Under pressure from her sisters to visit their mother during Christmas vacation, Vivian came into one of our sessions looking for ways to instrument a change in their relationship without unduly stressing herself. "I don't like Christmas anyway," she said truculently, then expressing the desire to "skip the whole family thing," as she had done for the past several years. But I reminded her that she had already decided to break with her habitual behavior, and courageously try something new.

We then discussed a range of experiments that Vivian might attempt for the Christmas holiday—all the way from only making a phone call to her mother, to staying with her at home for a few days. Vivian quickly decided that the first option was not sufficient to please anyone, and would fall far short of a truly courageous self-challenge. But she also felt that the second option—which her mother and sisters clearly wanted her to do—would violate her current need for privacy and "lots of space," as she always put it. It would be uncaring and unfair to "little Vivian," as she usually referred to her inner self.

We finally narrowed Vivian's list of possible experiments to one that seemed practical to her—to find a hotel room in her hometown and visit her mother for a few hours each day without sleeping over at home. She informed her family of this decision by telephone, and while no one was entirely pleased by her decision, they all agreed it was preferable to the total lack of communication that had gone before. The visit came off reasonably well, Vivian told me afterward, with both good moments and bad. But the most important reward was that regular communication was reestablished between Vivian and her mother—without Vivian having to back off her commitment to "little Vivian."

This case history demonstrates the importance of a judicious choice of attitude and action experiments. It's necessary to try something sufficiently challenging so that you really learn and grow from the experience, but it's important not to bite off more than you can chew. To try to change too rapidly is to be disrespectful to your own discomfort, which has a message for you about your limits and potentials at any given point in time. The advice of an experienced guide can help considerably in designing experiments that have a reasonable chance of success, although they must ultimately be undertaken at your own initiative. No value-driven experiment can be a total failure, because you will always be building and exemplifying your integrity and courage with every attempt.

4. **Rehearse your experiments in your mind, in a journal, on tape, or with supportive friends or a self-change guide.** This is a step that might not occur to people who instinctively initiate their own self-change experiments, but it can be a crucial one for many kinds of attempts. It's particularly important for all forms of communication experiments, such as requiring greater respect from someone important to you, expressing more affection to a spouse, or confiding in a friend to break your habit of withholding. To take on such attempts without

rehearsals is to run a great risk of putting on a tongue-tied debut, which may confuse other people and give yourself an unnecessary experience of failure.

In guided self-change sessions, I sometimes use the technique called "role-playing" to help people rehearse their chosen experiments in communication. In conventional therapy, role-playing is generally used as a means of instrumenting insight during sessions. In guided self-change, role-playing is a "dress rehearsal" for the real thing. It may yield considerable insight during a session, but it also has a real-world application.

For instance, after a client has practiced telling his wife (as played by me) a secret he has been keeping from her, he is then going home to tell his real wife the same thing. If he uncovers an important insight while rehearsing his confession to me, that's wonderful. But he can also take that insight home, when he feels ready (or almost ready, which is often as close as one can get), and use it to accelerate a real change in relationship.

Rehearsals can take many forms, of course, and can be as creatively designed as the attitude and behavior experiments themselves. They may be done solo, with the use of a mirror or journal. In much the same way that athletes can improve their game performances with mental rehearsals, any person pursuing self-change can boost their chances for success by assiduously "going through the motions" of their value-driven experiments, incorporating as many realistic aspects of the actual situation as possible. In a reverse role-playing process, a self-change guide can model ways to handle a situation for a client's consideration. This not only increases the client's range of options; it can also stir up latent feelings that may be examined before a change experiment takes places in the real world.

5. **Use your courage to implement your rehearsed experiment in attitude or behavior**. Perhaps because of the surplus of unrealistic, violent adventure films and TV shows in our society, we tend to have some strange ideas about what courage is. We may equate it with a Rambo-style attitude of being tough and well-armed—impassive and remote up until a crucial moment of decision, and then efficiently brutal thereafter. If we ever question ourselves about our courage, it is likely to be in terms of our capacity for physical warfare: Would we have the nerve to defend ourselves against an attacker? Would we give our lives for family or country?

In all but the most violent environments, however, everyone has much more need of the courage to change oneself than the bravado of self-defense. A more relevant question to be asking ourselves nowadays is: *Are we willing to give up destructive habits of attitude and behavior for our family, our country, and our own inner spirit?* If so, we have initiated a true and still-rare bravery.

Courage is simply willingness in action—the willingness to do what we know in our heart is right, despite any difficulties or fears we may encounter. Courage is signified less by leaping into enemy fire than by taking the tiniest initial step against one's own resistance to evolution. And courage arises from realizing fear is not an enemy to be destroyed, but an energy to be transformed and put to good use. Otherwise fear serves only as a bully holding us in place—unchanged, unhappy, and miserably ''safe.''

Max was a 52-year-old partner in an architectural firm who was living in an almost total paralysis when he was referred to me by his firm. It was not Max's limbs that were paralyzed, however—it was his will. After his wife had left him several years before, Max had gradually become immobilized by powerful feelings of worthlessness. Facing his co-workers eventually became so difficult that he simply stopped going to the office, calling weekly instead to say either that he was ill or, more honestly, that he ''just couldn't make it.'' At home he spent his time worrying intensely about the work he couldn't face, and going round and round in the same circles of thought about all that might be wrong with him.

Max's year-long psychotherapy was being paid for by his firm, but had not yielded any discernible results at work. His immediate supervisor Al had worked with Max for many years, and he had been involved in the decision to retain a change-oriented counselor. Of course Al was concerned about the work that constantly had to be rearranged or even turned away due to Max's chronic absences, but he was equally concerned about his friend's suffering, and the inexplicable collapse of will in a talented and still-young colleague.

In my first couple of sessions with Max, I got acquainted with his emotional history, and we discussed the range of feelings he was experiencing in his recent limbo. But we also talked about the application of the four basic values to his situation, and it soon became clear to Max that his avoidance of work was damaging his self-respect. Whatever had first caused him to feel inadequate could not really be blamed for all his subsequent retreats from responsibility; they had simply become a habit that reinforced his growing sense of unworthiness. To reverse that habit, Max was going to have to undertake an experiment in self-respect.

After we discussed a number of possibilities in our third session—a month after our first meeting—Max decided that he would try to go into the office the following week, and talk to Al about the work that was presently on the agenda. If he felt that he couldn't take anything on, he would at least help Al organize the situation, rather than continue to leave the firm waiting in suspense to hear whether Max might be able to contribute in the near future. Max made this decision to deal straightforwardly after I helped him recognize how unfair he was being to his colleagues and clients by his unpredictable participation.

In our session together, we role-played Max's upcoming meeting with Al; he was visibly nervous in his rehearsal, and I congratulated him for having the courage simply to imagine and practice a self-respecting act in the midst of so much fear and emotional pain. But it was obvious that the real challenge for Max remained outside my office.

The first report on Max's real-world experiment came not from him, but from Al. It turned out that Max had changed the experiment at the last minute, and invited Al out to lunch instead to discuss the situation at work. Although Max was unable to make any solid promises, he revealed to his partner much more of his feelings than he had before, and he let him know of his commitment to find a way back to fulfilling his responsibilities. This was news, of course—Max was usually making excuses to Al about why he was going to be absent yet again. For Al, this meeting was a dramatic sign that his colleague was already on his way back—so dramatic that he called me on the same afternoon of the lunch meeting, to ask what I had done to bring about this change.

Of course, I had done very little except to help Max view his situation in terms of the basic values that could reconnect him with his spiritual vitality— the source of the courage he needed to initiate an experiment in self-respect. The next time we met, I asked Max how difficult it had been to show up for the lunch appointment. "Oh, that wasn't hard at all," he remarked. "In fact, I kind of enjoyed it. What was really tough was calling Al to invite him."

"Oh, really?" I said. "On a scale of ten, how tough was it? Eight? Nine?"

Max smiled weakly and said, "Eleven. I was terrified."

At this point I reminded Max to collect the self-respect payoff he had earned by going ahead and doing what he believed was fair and right, despite his "eleven" level of anxiety. So many people do things despite their fears, yet unfairly deprive themselves of the credit they deserve for their courage. They feel they shouldn't have been afraid in the first place.

An intriguing postscript to this story is that a few weeks later, Max spontaneously began making lunch appointments with some of his firm's clients, talking to them about the progress of their projects and giving advice in the fashion of an outside consultant. Afterward, he would review with Al the substance of the meetings. It began to appear that Max's creative spirit was leading him back to work in a way that no one could have planned or imagined—a way that was healing to his extreme emotional vulnerability, allowing him to gradually rebuild confidence in his ability to relate without jumping abruptly back into a high-pressure office situation.

If we summon our deep inner spirit to "consult" on our toughest dilemmas—by enacting the values of respect, understanding, caring and fairness—it will lead us into creative solutions that are beyond the ken of our strictly rational mind. The logical way of thinking may tell us to "just get over it" when we are emotionally paralyzed or terrified, but purely rational solutions are doomed to failure without compassion for our fear and pain. Entwined with that compassion is true courage: the willingness to change, despite discomfort, for the sake of heartfelt values—rather than attack oneself or others because we feel unhappy.

6. **Commit yourself to repeated practice of new attitudes and actions.** A single courageous experiment is usually insufficient to establish momentum in the process of self-change. We need to make repeated attempts to establish value-driven behaviors and attitudes. Of course, experiments must change and evolve to fit our changing lives, and so we may never repeat any particular experiment in exactly the same form. But the fundamental *intent* of

experiments should remain consistent until substantial change has been accomplished—by which time new realms for change will surely have become evident.

In Max's case, meeting with Al to share the intent to come out of his professional limbo was a complete reversal of form, a courageous leap over a major hurdle. That did not mean, however, that his subsequent meetings with clients were effortlessly undertaken. He still had to struggle with his feelings of inadequacy, his fears, and his habit of inertia. And he had to remind himself frequently of *why* he was confronting his extreme awkwardness: not just to go back to work like a "normal" person, but to regain his place in the world with a foundation of self-respect. Having cleared the first hurdle, he could draw on the experience of success—the only real source of confidence—for subsequent challenges. But deliberate and consistent *practice* of his new, value-driven behavior was absolutely necessary for Max to break out of his self-destructive habit of paralysis.

One way to guarantee practice is to place yourself in situations in which it would be difficult or humiliating not to act in the new ways chosen. For instance, if you're trying to increase your confidence in group situations and have successfully completed an experiment of speaking out at a meeting, you can pursue repetitions of that experiment by enrolling in a public speaking class. Or, you may announce and describe your self-change experiments to a few close friends who will be curious enough to inquire about their progress. You may even come to an agreement with a friend you trust to carry out some experiments together.

I've mentioned several times the usefulness of keeping a journal in the process of self-change, and it has a great significance at this step of the work. Over the one to two years that a fundamental change in self-concept requires, it's extremely helpful to have an ongoing record of feelings, thoughts, decisions and experiments. Without it, we have a tendency to forget just how far we have come, and thus deprive ourselves of well-deserved pride in our accomplishments. With a means for looking back to where our self-change process began, we may be astonished to see how far beyond our initial goals we have progressed, and what unexpected and creative turns we took because we allowed our native spirit to re-energize us.

There are other means of record-keeping than writing in a journal, of course; intimate friendships of long duration will provide us with telling feedback on our self-change process, and those who are artists of any sort will naturally detect changes in their forms of expression. In Chapter 5, "Inside the Self-Change Consultation," I present a detailed discussion of another method for keeping track of one's growth in the context of guided self-change: the tape-recording of all self-change sessions, for the client's possession and review only. This enables the self-change client to own and evaluate the history of the counseling relationship, which is a valuable part of his personal evolution. It also gives him a direct, reliable means of evaluating the quality of the guidance he has paid for. Anyone who has been in conventional therapy will appreciate how unusual this practice is, and virtually everyone I've counseled will enthusiastically vouch for its usefulness. It is the most important technical feature of guided self-change, and I sincerely hope that it becomes standard practice for intensive personal-change counseling relationships.

7. **Rejoice and reward yourself each time you have been courageous and completed a self-change experiment—regardless of its success or failure.** How many of the people you know in therapy seem confident that they are on an expertly-guided path to changing and feeling significantly better about themselves? And how many of them just seem absorbed by their problems? The reason that the latter situation is common in conventional therapy is that therapy discourages real action by "patients" until the course of treatment is completed—and that can take years.

By contrast, guided self-change encourages value-driven action as soon as the client can come up with an experiment that she feels is reasonably challenging and worthwhile. The guide can help her dream up this experiment and rehearse it, and heartily encourage her to enact it in the "real world" outside and between guided self-change consultations. And whether or not her experiment initially accomplishes its goals, the guide will congratulate his client on her courageous attempt to change—thereby modeling for her the appreciation she should afford herself, regardless of any experiment's success or failure.

Let's say that a young woman is attempting to establish a relationship of greater mutual respect with her husband, and has decided to challenge his habit of subtly ridiculing her intellect at dinner parties with their friends. She devises an experiment with two steps: First, she will inform her husband in private that she will call attention to his ridiculing behavior the next time it occurs, instead of suffering silent embarrassment as she has always done before. This gives them the opportunity to discuss the problem in a fair manner, while putting both of them on notice that she intends to take action publicly as well. The first part of the experiment comes off without a hitch—the woman's husband acknowledges his behavior and promises to act more respectfully in the future. But when she calls him on a denigrating remark he makes at their next social occasion, he laughs her off and no one seems to notice her point.

If I heard such a report in a guided self-change session, I would encourage my client to balance her natural feeling of disappointment with some well-deserved pride for completing her self-change experiment as planned. She may not have solved the whole problem of disrespect in relationship to her husband, but she has already progressed from being a passive victim of unfair treatment to an active agent of responsible change. She has served her spirit well and she really deserves to feel self-respect and some joy for her courage, despite the fact that a serious problem persists and will require further action experiments to be mitigated.

If she courageously refuses to retreat, her husband will come to realize that he must treat her with the same high standards of respect and caring that she offers him, if they are to remain together. And her spirit will increasingly rejoice that she is finally listening and responding to its cries for help.

When we become too result-oriented, we can lose sight of our inner progress toward change, and thus fail to celebrate our advances. This not only deprives us of feeling better about ourselves, but it also deprives us of the patience necessary to bring about substantial change in the most difficult problems.

The Long Haul of Change

Celebrating our inner growth not only affords us the patience that it takes to change our personalities and relationships; it also establishes a positive context in which to receive an unpredictable variety of feelings that will arise once the process of self-change has established its own momentum. It doesn't take too many consciously derived experiments implementing respect, understanding, caring, and fairness before one's inner creative spirit begins to manifest and accelerate the process of change. Then we may begin to experience all the insights and catharsis we can handle—much more so, according to my experience and observation, than in conventional therapy, which restricts itself to summoning insight and catharsis before expecting any real change to be undertaken.

The reason for this is simple. To act deliberately in a self-respecting way when one's personality is steeped in disrespect will begin to "dredge up" buried attitudes and feelings that have contributed to the personality's negativity. Because new attitudes and actions have proven that the old ways were not inevitable, useful questions spontaneously arise: *"Why have I been living in this painful way for so long? What experiences and feelings kept me so stuck?"* The homeostasis of living in a negative feeling state has been disrupted, and the resultant crisis provides an opportunity to seek a new equilibrium based on positive feelings.

Celebrating this shift whenever appropriate is the best way to speed up the process, and it is a uniquely human celebration. To my knowledge, no other animal has the capacity to dramatically alter its fundamental awareness through compassionate self-observation and courageous experimentation—turning self-hatred into respect and despair into joy.

Over the long haul of self-change, we really do get the chance to transform our fears into courage—and thus change our problems into opportunities. We also embark upon a journey that can take us to places we never even dreamed we could visit, back when our self-limiting personality was keeping our infinitely creative spirit out of the picture. The process of letting it back in will never be effortless, but neither should it be a dreary struggle. In the next part of this book, we'll take a detailed look at how guided self-change honors and calls forth one's natural, spiritual creativity. But first it's necessary to understand why existing therapeutic systems fail to do just that—and why so many people in therapy actually change so little.

PART II

FINDING A GUIDE TO
HELP YOU CHANGE

The Woman Who Stole To Care

When I first met Ellen, she was a very troubled 21-year-old sent to me by her parents, whom I had been counseling for their considerable marital difficulties. Ellen's father was a middle-level corporate executive who drank too much and was traveling most of the time; he and his wife endured a sexless and argumentative relationship. Despite the fact that I had been mostly unsuccessful in encouraging them to improve their ways of living and relating, Ellen's parents thought I might be able to help their daughter reverse her recent slide into chaos.

A drug-using high school drop-out, Ellen was unable to live on her own for very long, as she bounced from job to job, ran up numerous traffic violations, and seemed constantly on the verge of deeper trouble with the law because of her drug and alcohol consumption. Although she had a number of casual and rather disreputable friends, she was intimate with no one and often acted the part of a tough, streetwise loner. The last time Ellen had been evicted from an apartment and ended up living at home again, her parents insisted that she come to see me. This was not the best beginning for a self-change process, but I promised Ellen's parents I'd do my best.

Nervous, unkempt, and dangerously thin, Ellen came into her first session with an obvious chip on her shoulder. Knowing what her home situation was like, I understood that this young woman must be carrying an immense amount of pain inside, and I took a tender, nonconfrontive approach in the hope of getting her to open up a little. Besides expressing contempt for her parents, however, she said little that was revealing until the end of the session, when she blurted out, "My parents don't even know the worst thing I do. And I do it all the time."

"What's that?" I asked.

"I steal," Ellen replied. "Couple of times a week ever since I was fifteen. Mostly tapes and CDs, you know, music stuff. I've worked at a lot of record stores and I really rip them off." She then looked at me innocently and paused before adding, "But I don't keep most of it. I give it away to my friends."

As I would learn over the next few sessions, Ellen was indeed a consummate shoplifter. She was also apparently a superb salesperson, which explained why she easily found employment despite being frequently dismissed. Although she had never been caught stealing at work, she had been let go a number of times because of store owners' suspicions. She had no secret desire to get caught, and she was smart enough to elude certain detection.

All this I learned during the first three sessions with Ellen, who related almost everything in tones of anger while seldom revealing the hurt that festered beneath it. I talked quite a bit too, introducing Ellen to the four values of respect, understanding, caring, and fairness that she could use as guidelines for changing her way of life. I also asked her repeatedly how she felt when she stole and when she abused drugs, and if she could imagine what it would feel like to live a straight, productive life.

But it seemed as if Ellen could hardly hear me, insulated as she was in her armor of contempt and fearful arrogance. Every time I gave her the tapes of our sessions, I knew it was unlikely she would review them afterward. Although she kept coming back, she gave me no signs of willingness to commit to looking seriously at her life and trying out new possibilities.

Finally, near the end of our third session, I practically begged her to listen to the session tapes: "Look, you can listen to them just so you can tell me how I'm all wrong about everything. That would be a start. But we're not going to get anywhere unless you're willing to participate."

Ellen shrugged her shoulders nonchalantly and left. When she came back several weeks later and made some feeble excuses for not having reviewed her tape, I warned her that I had some strong feelings about her and her life, and needed to say a few things in a loud voice. To do this, I would stand at the far side of the room so as not to threaten her.

"You can leave anytime you want," I said. "I'm not going to yell at you, but I do have to give you an idea of how frustrating and painful it is for me to continue seeing you. I feel like I'm going through the motions as if something worthwhile were happening, and taking your parents' money while you and I know nothing is being accomplished.

"If you can steal and look yourself in the mirror and feel good about yourself, then please don't waste any more of my time or your parents' money. If you can actually feel good as a crook, then what I have to say is useless. But I'll just bet that no matter how exciting it is to steal—and I'm sure it's very exciting—afterward you don't have any satisfaction about the stuff you've got, you hate yourself for doing it, and you end up promising yourself you'll never do it again."

By now Ellen looked a little shocked. But I felt I was finally getting her attention, so I continued:

"If I'm wrong about all this, fire me. But I can't stand what you're doing to yourself, and it's too painful for me to witness anymore. I hope you'll take this session tape home and just listen to my little speech here again. If you decide that I'm full of it, fine. But find the guts somewhere to take an honest look and decide whether I've got it right.

"Then if you decide you want to do something to change how you act, and how you feel about yourself, then I will be *delighted* to work with you for as long as it takes. If you have to leave your family behind to get healthy, I'll support you in that. You may need a lot of support just to go your own way, or who knows—you may become an inspiration to your family. But I'm absolutely certain, Ellen, that you have the intelligence, sensitivity, and courage to change. You're the one to decide whether you can face your fears and risk feeling good about yourself."

Although I knew I was running the risk of driving Ellen out of counseling, I wasn't bluffing. Every word I said had arisen from my own allegiance to the values I espouse and believe in—and from my sense of Ellen's strength, vulnerability, and gifts. It turned out that I was right about Ellen's courage, because she had enough to return after that session, having reviewed the tape of it. Over the next few meetings, her long-standing anger began to alternate with grieving and tears, as Ellen told me many stories of how she had failed to get understanding and encouragement from her parents. I had to be patient with her desire to blame them for everything for a while, but at least we had contacted Ellen's real feelings. (The most difficult thing for self-doubting people to learn is compassion for their wounded inner child, in order to get past anger at their parents.) I was able to tell Ellen then how much I appreciated her trust in telling me about her pain and vulnerability.

And as we talked about what kind of life Ellen might build for herself, she gradually began to admit her ambitions to work in popular music—not as a musician, but in publicity for record companies and performers. Thus we both began to understand some of the distorted desires behind her criminal activity. Ellen also admitted that she gave away all her booty as a means to gain prestige among her friends. She felt satisfaction from giving away what she stole, not in keeping it.

"What else could it mean," I asked her one day, "that you would rather give the stuff away than keep it?"

"Oh, I don't know, it makes me feel important," she said.

"Well, it also seems to me like a self-hating but heartfelt way to care about people," I suggested.

Tears sprang to Ellen's eyes and she said, "You mean I could be trying to do something good?"

"It sure looks that way to me, but only you can look inside and see if it might be true."

Ellen was silent for a few minutes, and I could see her terrible awkwardness in having to feel anything good about herself. Just as she lacked compassion for her pain, she was not allowing herself any feelings of positive worth—because they would have been inconsistent with her all-powerful self-hatred. The idea of looking for a feeling of self-respect inside was quite foreign to her. It was a revelation to her that such a value could exist within her, as something she could use to determine the rightness of her decisions and actions.

By the end of this session, Ellen was ready to undertake an experiment to quit using drugs, which came rather easily to her since she had quit for short periods before. In our next session, I suggested that Ellen try not to steal before we met again—not as a moral issue, but simply in order to see what kinds of feelings would be stirred up as a result.

"Well, I know that stealing isn't right," she said.

"That's not the point," I reiterated. "What I want to know is, how will you *feel* if you look in the mirror after not stealing for a couple weeks? Forget about what your parents or the law would say. Maybe you could imagine you had a sister or daughter who had been stealing, and managed to quit. Do you think you'd be proud of her? Could you handle feeling that much respect for yourself?"

Ellen responded to those questions with a confused look, but she left the session agreeing to consider the new experiment. She managed to go ten days without stealing, the longest period in years, after thousands of thefts. In our next session, she told me how flabbergasted she was when she stole after that ten-day period and felt "just awful"—she literally became sick to her stomach.

This was the beginning of the end of Ellen's shoplifting habit. She stole once or twice more over the next month, and then never again. Two years after we first met, she says now that "someone would have to kidnap my best friend or blackmail me to get me to steal"—it has simply lost all attraction for her, as her distorted ways of attaining self-respect and giving care have been gradually replaced with direct and healthy expressions.

Enrolled in junior college and maintaining a 3.5 grade average, Ellen is enthusiastically involved in her studies and has begun working part time at an entry-level job in a recording studio. Her shift in lifestyle has cost her many of her former friends, and she is still reluctant to become involved in any intimate relationship, feeling that she must take one thing at a time in her growth process. Still often lonely, she struggles to stay on speaking terms with her parents—whom she once ordered to leave her apartment because they brought their fighting to dinner in her home.

Because her parents still pay for her self-change consultations, Ellen has limited our contacts to brief phone calls for the last six months. Yet I knew she was well on the way to her new life when she missed one of her appointments—because she was so busy with school that she forgot it.

I think I did help Ellen see herself in a new way, and I introduced her to the idea of self-respect as a vital aspect of her deep inner nature, and as a crucial guideline for her life. I told her many times, in fact, that I was dedicated to serving as an advocate for her inner spirit. But it must be said that Ellen did the vast majority of the hard work needed to change her life. Our sessions were never closer together than once every two weeks, and usually occurred monthly. After only eight sessions over four months, Ellen had stopped drug use and shoplifting; thereafter, her progress was even more rapid.

It's almost unheard-of for people like Ellen to change their ways without court-ordered therapy and the threat of jail. Even then it would be a rarity for law-abiding behavior to be sustained once probation was lifted. In my own practice, people who make changes as substantial and rapid as Ellen's are definitely in the minority. But the research on psychotherapy shows that it achieves, at best, some reduction of symptoms in cases like Ellen's. Seldom does it result in fundamental changes in self-concept.

I know that such change is possible, however, because I've seen it in dozens of people I've coached. The secret is to call forth a client's own self-healing capacity by helping her relearn the values of respect, understanding, caring, and fairness—in relation to herself as well as others. Once that process gains its own natural momentum, all a self-change guide has to do is stand on the sidelines and provide some cheerleading. Ellen's progress always reminds me of the saying, ''Pity the poor teacher who is not surpassed by his students.'' In this case, I truly deserve no pity.

CHAPTER 4:

The Limitations of Psychotherapy

. . . much will be gained if we succeed in transforming your hysterical misery into common unhappiness.
—Sigmund Freud

Consider the following case history of an "atypical depression," appearing in a recent issue of the Harvard Medical School's *Mental Health Letter*:

> *A single woman in her thirties comes to a clinic and says that for several months she has been feeling sad and hopeless and too anxious to concentrate at work. She fears that she will lose her job, and occasionally has thoughts of suicide. She has gained 15 pounds and is constantly tired; she has trouble falling asleep and then sleeps through her alarm. Often she finds herself bursting into tears with her heart pounding. The symptoms began when a boyfriend left her. Her self-esteem has always been low, and she has had previous episodes of depression, usually brought on by disappointments in love. At times she has taken diet pills and drunk heavily, although she is now avoiding drugs and alcohol. She says that her mother used to have similar feelings. She does not improve when given imipramine, a standard tricyclic antidepressant, but recovers in a few weeks when switched to another type of drug, phenelzine, a mono-amine oxidase (MAO) inhibitor.*

What's missing from this story? It's easy to notice that this case history fails to discuss the depth or

duration of the woman's drug-induced "recovery."
Did the medication permanently relieve her feelings
of sadness, hopelessness, and anxiety? Did it also
cure her fatigue, sleeping disturbances, overeating,
weeping attacks and suicidal thinking? Did it restore
her self-esteem and enable her to find a rewarding
intimate relationship? Most important of all, how
will she fare if she stops taking the "MAO inhibi-
tor"? Or will she be forever dependent on a mood-
altering medication in order to cope with her un-
satisfying life?

The suspicion that this woman's recovery may not
be as simple as first described is confirmed in the
conclusion of the article discussing this case history:

> The practical usefulness of a diagnosis of atypical depression has
> not been established. Whatever a patient's symptoms, most psy-
> chiatrists will try other drugs before prescribing MAO inhibi-
> tors, because they can produce serious side effects, including
> drowsiness, dizziness, insomnia, and, when combined with cer-
> tain foods . . . a sudden rise in blood pressure. Long-term psy-
> chotherapy is often helpful for people who have mixed
> symptoms, rapidly cycling moods, or depression with symptoms
> that resemble a personality disorder. Patients suffering from
> phobias or compulsive rituals may need behavioral treatment as
> well as drugs. Psychotherapy along with drug treatment is
> often better than either alone.

This passage reveals two sobering admissions:
that the woman's diagnosis—on which all subsequent treatment must be based—is of questionable
usefulness, and that the drug she was given has significant side effects. But it is even more remarkable
for what it omits. There is no discussion here (nor
in the remainder of the article) of how the woman

under treatment could be encouraged to undertake the kind of self-directed personal growth that could permanently decrease her susceptibility to depression and reduce her need for drugs. As a psychiatric patient, she is regarded primarily as a presenter of symptoms that are to be eliminated. In this view, "mental health" amounts to little more than the absence of symptoms and pathological behaviors.

Such shortcomings of psychiatric treatment (and psychotherapy) have been elaborated upon by a growing number of critics over the last several decades. The criticism has ranged from opposition to specific psychiatric interventions (such as electroshock treatment), to attacks on the foundations of psychoanalytic theory, to a basic questioning about whether psychotherapy should be viewed as a medical treatment.

In fact, another recent issue of the Harvard *Mental Health Letter* carried an article entitled "Psychoanalysis: The Second Century," in which author Robert Michels, M.D. noted that:

> *Psychoanalysis is now becoming less exclusively medical even in the United States . . . In the second century of psychoanalysis, the question will no longer be whether its practitioners have to be physicians, but whether they need to be members of organized health professions at all.*

If therapists are not to be doctors in the future, then what should they be? And how should they practice? To answer these questions, we have to look into the past, to find the deeper roots of psychological healing.

From Philosophy to Medicine

Today's typical "therapy consumer" might be surprised to learn that the true roots of psychotherapy lie in religion and philosophy, not medical science. As psychiatrist Thomas Szasz wrote in *The Myth of Psychotherapy*, "psychotherapy is a modern, scientific-sounding name for what used to be called the 'cure of souls.' The true history of psychiatry thus begins not with the early nineteenth-century psychiatrists, but with the Greek philosophers and the Jewish rabbis of antiquity; and it continues with the Catholic priests and Protestant pastors, over a period of nearly two millennia, before the medical soul-doctors appear on the stage of history."

Szasz is not the first to argue that we have misplaced the "cure of souls" in the realm of medicine. Carl Jung split with his mentor Freud over the spiritual significance of psychological experience, once observing that he had not treated a single patient in the second half of life whose real problem was not essentially a religious one. As a pragmatic coach of change, I'm not interested in adding to the literature of this controversy. But I am interested in what works best for my clients, and that's why I make it clear from the outset that I no longer practice psychotherapy in the usual sense—as a treatment for "mental illness."

Instead, I work to help clients develop their own practical route to what the Greeks called *metanoia*: a change of mind. To begin that journey requires recognition of one's dissatisfaction with life, and dissatisfaction may involve extreme mental and emotional distress. But in most cases, I do not find it helpful to label the various forms of distress and dissatisfaction that my clients present as types of mental illness. This labeling slows down—and can even reverse—the process of changing minds and curing souls.

To label someone a "patient" with a diagnosable mental illness or disability is to reinforce the sense of inadequacy that most people feel when they reach the point of asking for professional help. In all but the most seriously and chronically disturbed people, this expert validation of a person's feeling of defectiveness interferes with the initiation of constructive changes in her attitudes, behaviors, and beliefs.

In his book *Love's Executioner*, psychotherapist Irvin D. Yalom reports on a critical moment from one of his case histories, when a client began to take responsibility for his antisocial behavior: "The tone of the session had changed. . . . We had grown deadly serious. I felt more like a philosophy or religious teacher than a therapist, but I knew that this was the proper trail."

This trail, that psychotherapy at its best sometimes stumbles upon, is the only proper path for the process I call guided self-change.

However, I should make it clear that my philosophical framework does not imply any set of religious or metaphysical beliefs about the nature of reality. For the purposes of the help I'm offering, my philosophy begins with my explicit statement of values; moves on to feelings as the messages of one's authentic nature; continues with my belief in courage as the primary catalyst of change; and ends with my practical support of the client's "inner spirit" as the source of her unique creativity, conscience, and capacity for love. I believe that this kind of philosophical stance represents the future of psychological counseling, for it returns "soul healing" to its proper realm. Its misplacement can be traced primarily to the legacy of the father of psychoanalysis and modern psychotherapy.

The Mixed Legacy of Freud

No one can doubt that Sigmund Freud radically altered the way in which modern Westerners understand themselves. He gave us not only the widely-accepted notion that our thoughts, feelings, and attitudes arise from two realms of the mind—the conscious and the unconscious—but also the idea that much of our adult behavior may be subconsciously influenced by very early childhood traumas.

Freud is also responsible for the popular image of psychotherapy as an encounter between a troubled person lying on a couch, talking obsessively to a fatherly, exceptionally intellectual man who listens acutely to his patient's woes, all the while taking notes and speaking rarely. This is an image, of course, that is nowadays more likely to be ridiculed than respected, and that accurately represents only the practice of a relatively small number of classical psychoanalysts.

Specific tenets of Freud's psychoanalytic theory have been under attack since his own day, and the criticism has only intensified in recent years. A critique of Freudian theory is beyond the scope of this book, but my perspective on his work is basically aligned with that of Szasz, who wrote in *The Myth of Psychotherapy* that Freud's treatment method was nothing more than "contrived and controlled conversation relabeled with the technicized terminology of his self-styled science."

Szasz is not necessarily saying that conversation is unhelpful or ineffective for people in psychological distress. He is saying, and I wholeheartedly agree, that conversation disguised as a science and a medical treatment is a fraud perpetrated on those who pay for it and place their faith in the process. When the medical image of "contrived and controlled conversation" is enhanced by a psychiatrist's power to prescribe mood-altering drugs, the disguise of the "mind doctor" becomes complete and virtually impenetrable.

Then, people seeking help to relieve their distress and manage their lives better are strongly tempted to believe that they have a "mental illness" which can only be cured by this kind of doctor. Simultaneously, they take on a new problem and give up much of the responsibility that is necessary to create and integrate new beliefs, attitudes, and behaviors. They exchange the considerable difficulty and potential of changing themselves—often because they do not understand that self-change is possible—for the expensive and extended process of submitting to another person's diagnosis and treatment of their problems.

These problems are then given new and impressive names. For instance, a person's chronic anger and self-destructive resentment may be labeled as "clinical depression"; a person who cannot sort out a variety of powerful and conflicting emotions may be diagnosed as having an "anxiety disorder." I do not deny that certain people seem predisposed to certain patterns of symptoms, but I prefer the term *condition* to *illness* for all such patterns of distress.

What we call mental illness is a breakdown of a human being's mental, emotional, *and* spiritual functioning, usually as a result of many factors operating at different levels: genetic, environmental, psychological, and physiological. But the idea of illness is associated with overt symptoms that are treatable only by medical intervention. As a result, psychotherapy and all the other healing professions remain seriously confused about the role of feelings, values, and spiritual resources in the art of living and healing.

Not all psychotherapies resort to extremes of medical mystification, and some, such as Rogerian therapy, rely on plainer language and a more egalitarian relationship between the therapist and the person seeking help (Carl Rogers was one of the first therapists to use the word "client" instead of "patient," in fact.). But they are all part of Freud's legacy to the extent that they identify psychological difficulties as illness, and that they confer on the therapist the identity of a scientifically-trained "healer." From such fundamental assumptions of psychotherapy arise all of its major limitations.

Six Problems

My experience as a conventionally-trained psychiatrist who chose to become a self-change guide has made clear to me six major problems of contemporary psychotherapeutic practice. I review them briefly here not for the sake of adding to the antitherapy literature, but for the benefit of several kinds of readers: those who may be seeking psychological counseling for the first time; those who are dissatisfied with counseling they are presently receiving; or those who have derived benefit from past therapy and now would like to work on a particular aspect of their lives without submitting to a dependent, time-consuming relationship with a therapist to accomplish their goal.

Unfortunately, psychotherapists seldom if ever disclose the limitations of their approach to their clients at the outset of counseling. This is due largely to the implicit belief that psychotherapy is unquestionably The Answer for people with psychological problems, and the further assumption that people seeking psychological help are incapable of assessing the pros and cons of psychotherapy itself. But clients have the right to request a full disclosure of the potential drawbacks and "side effects" of psychotherapy before they contract for it, just as they should request disclosures from medical doctors before surgery or treatment with drugs. (For a disclosure of the limitations of self-change guidance, see Chapter 7, "When is Therapy Appropriate?")

People about to contract for psychotherapy should consider the following major problem areas of that mode of treatment:

1. *The imposition of a diagnosis of mental illness or emotional disorder;*

2. *The absence of values as an explicit guidance system for psychological healing and growth;*

3. *The reliance on a dependent professional relationship as a guidance system;*

4. *The discouragement of life-changing experimentation on the client's part until a course of treatment is completed;*

5. *The failure to recognize the client's inner spiritual resources—talents, energies, and feelings—as the only dependable source of change;*

6. *A tendency to view the client's potential in limited, pessimistic terms.*

1. **The imposition of a medical diagnosis** on people seeking counseling has obvious consequences that have already been discussed briefly in this chapter, but there are less apparent implications that are worth mentioning as well. Foremost among these is the *negation of feelings* that a diagnosis tends to produce. As discussed in Chapter 2, feelings are best understood as vital messages from one's deep inner self—messages that may be seriously distorted and quite difficult to decode, but messages that can point the way to self-acceptance and growth nonetheless. The work of comprehending and "owning" one's feelings is hard enough when one is consciously and positively engaged in that process. It becomes virtually impossible when one is receiving professional encouragement to regard difficult feel-

ings as further manifestations of an official disorder.

Additionally, a medical diagnosis can induce in a troubled person a fascination with suffering. Rather than ennobling the client by recognizing and calling out his inner potential for change, the therapist may inadvertently ennoble the client's difficulties and encourage an addiction to being impaired. A diagnosis that sounds complicated and somewhat mysterious thus becomes part of the client's identity, and his fascination with it makes his underlying difficulties all the more difficult to resolve.

This is the unfunny side of the "Woody Allen syndrome," when a person identifies himself as a hopeless "neurotic" rather than a courageous human being seeking to lessen his suffering by changing his ways of being. I have seen this syndrome in action in mental hospitals, where patients are more likely to introduce themselves by their diagnoses ("Hello, I'm a manic-depressive") than by their names!

2. **The absence of values** in psychotherapy makes it work like a ship without a rudder. Its pathological bias orients therapy toward the elimination of symptoms rather than the encouragement of growth. Thus, therapy is much better at keeping one's ship afloat during a storm than in charting an overall course.

The lack of guiding values in therapy has to do with the identification of psychology in general as a science —science being a supposedly value-free investigation of objective reality. Putting aside the question of how often science is really conducted in this manner, it's obvious that psychological reality is a highly *subjective* realm. We cannot make important decisions or have rewarding relationships if we view ourselves as biological machines subject only to objective forces of nature. Our values may be distorted or unconscious, but we do act on the basis of ideas that we think are worth serving—whether those ideas relate only to our personal survival and comfort, or have a broader altruistic intent.

Therapists in training are generally taught that they should not *impose* their values on clients. This means, for example, that a heterosexual therapist should refrain from attempting to persuade a homosexual client that the therapist's sexual orientation is more "normal." If values are regarded only as such social guidelines, relying more on external approval than deep inner validation, then they will indeed be problematic as teaching and learning tools.

What is seldom considered is the possibility that clients and therapists can *mutually endorse* a set of basic values that will serve human beings well in all situations. I have settled on respect, understanding, caring, and fairness as such a set of universal values. In guided self-change relationships I do not impose these values on my clients, but I do ask them to endorse them by contract at the outset of counseling. If the client agrees to them, then we have mutually established a conscious sense of direction for problem-solving and growth experiments. If the client finds them disagreeable, then we know at the outset that I am not the right person to serve as his counselor. If the client is not sure what these values mean, then I am willing to discuss them at length so that we can arrive at a consensus about their meaning before we sign a contract for counseling.

3. **The reliance on a therapeutic relationship for guidance** is one of the most insidious faults of psychotherapy, one that leads both to outright abuses and to more subtle disservices. Because the supposedly medical perspective of psychotherapy cannot help but get mixed up with philosophical and spiritual questions in the consulting room, therapists come to be regarded not merely as mind doctors but also as nonreligious sources of wisdom. It has often been observed that psychotherapists serve as spiritual counselors for modern sophisticates who have consciously rejected religion as a reliable system of values and morals.

The problem is that the typical psychotherapist's "religion" is the science of psychology, which means that his view of reality will tend to be excessively intellectual and analytic. It will also impose a set of hidden values inherent to a particular mode of therapy. When a client sorely needs to reestablish a practical sense of her inner spiritual "knowing" as a means to sort out chaotic feelings, she will instead be influenced to become ever more "rational" as a means of minimizing their effect.

If a client is not subconsciously regarding the therapist as a spiritual teacher, then she will almost certainly look upon him as an ersatz parent, someone whose approval counts for more than the client's own self-validation. This dependent and unequal relationship is both expected and generally encouraged to develop in psychotherapy, and is officially labeled as "the transference." (For a more detailed discussion, see Chapter 5.)

In his book *Children of Psychiatrists and Other Psychotherapists*, Thomas Maeder succinctly describes how the transference begins to "fill in" for a client's continuing inability to relate healthily to self and others:

> The particular danger to the patient against which therapists must be vigilant, but often are not, is that the therapy begins to settle in as part of the patient's life rather than remaining an active process whereby he can integrate himself into living. The patient may begin to look forward to sessions and live his life for the unacknowledged purpose of interesting and pleasing the therapist. Problems may be apparently resolved and changes made because the patient feels that is what the therapist wants, and have no profound or permanent effect because performed more for the dramatic value or the therapist's approval than from a sense of inner need.

As you'll see in the next chapter, the system of guided self-change has several safeguards against the development of such a dependent and un-productive relationship. Basically, guided self-change minimizes the transference in part by establishing an egalitarian relationship between the client and his "change coach." Constantly encouraged to risk self-respecting experiments in attitudes and behavior, the client can build his self-esteem through tangible successes in the real world, rather than relying on a therapist's analysis and approval of his progress.

4. **The discouragement of life-changing experimentation by the client** in therapy is related, once again, to the medical bias of this kind of counseling. A "patient" who is seen as ill or defective cannot be expected to make substantial changes in his way of life until he is "cured" by analysis and treatment.

The problem, of course, is that analysis may go on for years and years without any substantial improvements in the patient's way of life and self-acceptance. If drug treatment is involved, it will tend to cloud a patient's rational mind and numb his feelings—the very data he should be learning to decipher in order to take better care of himself.

That is not to say that analysis achieves nothing. Many veterans of therapy develop a greater understanding of their unhappiness than they had before entering therapy. They may conclude, quite rightly, that the original source of their unhappiness was unfair, incompetent, or even cruel treatment at the hands of their parents during childhood. And then they may decide that there is nothing that can be done about what Freud called such a "common unhappiness."

In fact, people in therapy may find themselves explicitly discouraged by their therapist from acting in new ways outside sessions, because it has been observed that analysis brings up strong feelings that may result in destructive or erratic actions outside the consulting room (usually referred to by therapists as "acting out"). The reason that this happens is that therapy clients are given no coaching on how to manage strong feelings in accord with values that protect oneself and others.

As you will see in the next chapter, one of the most valuable services a self-change guide provides is the in-session *rehearsal* of value-driven change experiments that are later to be conducted on the outside, in the client's life. Rehearsal with a change coach gives people the opportunity to confront some of the feelings that come up as the process of self-understanding and change takes place. And since it is the guide's job to coach action, rather than discourage it, he can help the client choose the safest and most realistic experiments among all the possibilities.

In typical therapy, the consequence of discouraging new behaviors on the part of the client is quite predictable: The client learns how to change very slowly, if at all. He neither develops the courage to take necessary risks nor learns to make full use of the insights that therapy may have provided.

5. **The failure to recognize the client's inner spiritual resources** can deprive the client of contact with the only source of lasting guidance available in life, the "inner teacher" whose intuition and creativity far exceed that of the ordinary, rational mind. With the exception of the newer "transpersonal" therapies that address the issue of spiritual development, most of psychology disdains the idea of an inner teacher because it is overtly subjective and therefore unscientific and unquantifiable. Also, the route to attaining a steady sense of inner guidance is highly individualistic and unpredictable. Accepting this idea means accepting that the power of psychological healing and growth lies within the client's deep resources, rather than the therapist's techniques or wisdom.

As a self-change guide, I accept the idea of the inner teacher because I cannot ignore the evidence of its existence. This is not evidence that can be charted on a graph or assigned a degree of statistical significance, but I have seen it clearly in the changing lives of my courageous clients. I know that I can do little more for people than point the way toward their "real selves," and help them generate the courage to follow their feelings and values toward a life of inspired wholeness. A traditional psychotherapist might instead warn his clients away from "unrealistic expectations," because he is necessarily aware of the low success rates of his vocation. But I believe that says more about the potential of psychotherapy than the potentials of people seeking psychological help.

6. **The tendency to view the client's potential pessimistically** is the predictable consequence of a counseling approach that focuses on pathology. If you read many of the classic case histories of psychoanalysis, for instance, you will soon discover a tone of negativity that tinges nearly all of them, even the stories of apparent success. Hardly anyone thinks of psychotherapy as an inspiring field of endeavor wherein people are helped to rediscover their spiritual birthright of inner freedom, creativity, and fulfillment. Rather, it is generally seen as a field where esoterically-trained specialists of questionable personal stability help others to cope minimally with their overwhelming problems.

By honestly affirming the great inner potential of my clients in guided self-change, I am not espousing a blanket optimism that automatically works wonders with everyone who sees me. In fact, I have often terminated counseling with clients when it became clear that self-change guidance was proving unproductive—not because of any inherent flaws in my clients, but because I was unable to inspire them to pursue value-driven experiments in change. Unlike some psychotherapists, I will not indefinitely "take care" of people who see what they need to do in order to change and, out of fear or stubbornness, repeatedly refuse to act. This may seem hardhearted to some, but in fact it is a practical recognition of my limited capacity as a counselor and coach of change.

The Unpredictability of Change

Surprisingly, the direct affirmation of a client's potential may create considerable resistance to my guidance, leading to the sort of counseling relationship that a psychotherapist would probably find too frustrating or even humiliating to continue. I had such an experience with Marjorie, a woman in her late twenties who failed to show up for several initial appointments, finally agreeing to pay in advance as an added inducement to appear. Even then, she was half an hour late, having pulled off on a freeway shoulder to consider once more the pros and cons of meeting me.

Upon entering my office, Marjorie openly expressed her relief at finding that I had huge chairs, large enough to accommodate her extreme obesity. She admitted, in fact, that her very life was in peril from congestive heart failure threatened solely by her weight. Her other problems rapidly became clear: She was trapped in a dead-end job as a factory technician, she had yet to experience any kind of sexual intimacy in her life (or simple, affectionate petting, for that matter), and she had recently dropped out of the church that had once been a mainstay of her life. Marjorie had recently come to feel that she was so bad, dirty, and undeserving that she no longer had any right to talk to God.

By any psychotherapeutic standards, Marjorie's prognosis was very poor, and the seriousness of her problems would have required therapy sessions at least weekly for several years. In fact, I saw her more frequently than most of my clients for the first year of our relationship—though never more often than weekly—after which she began coming less often because of her discomfort during our meetings. The source of her discomfort: my consistently high opinion of Marjorie as an extraordinarily bright and sensitive person with a terrific potential for relationship and service to others. My view of her was so far removed from what she could accept about herself that Marjorie increasingly distanced herself from my encouragement, and to this day she says I might have been more helpful if I had been more conservative in expressing my positive regard. This was not possible, however, because my positive regard for Marjorie was utterly sincere: I reported to her only what I saw in her native spirit.

As it worked out, the less that Marjorie saw me, the more she actually changed. In her struggle to accept herself in small but increasing degrees, Marjorie undertook experiments to reduce her eating, help other people through volunteer work, and rejoin her church through group activities. Always fiercely disagreeing with me about her worth, Marjorie nonetheless began to discover it in the change experiments she undertook outside our sessions.

Three years after we met, Marjorie had curtailed

our professional appointments entirely, and only called me every now and then to let me know how she was doing. She eventually became engaged to a man she met at church, and began studying with him to undertake missionary work. By this time, her weight was down to a healthy level and her eating compulsion was well in control.

Can I claim Marjorie as a success story of guided self-change? I'm not sure, because she still doesn't entirely agree with my estimate of her talents— although as a result of her good works, she no longer sees herself as defective. And it's clear that she did most of the work to change her life. When real change occurs, that's the only way it can be. The most a guide can do is to provide encouragement, honest confrontation, and practical advice . . . and then get out of the way.

Beyond the Anti-Therapy Attitude

While I am in agreement with some contemporary critics of psychotherapeutic practice, I am deeply concerned about the lack of practical alternatives to therapy that they present. A good example of the typical anti-therapy attitude can be found in the controversial book *AGAINST THERAPY: Emotional Tyranny and the Myth of Psychological Healing*, by the scholar and former lay psychoanalyst Jeffrey M. Masson. In a work that aggressively calls for the "abolition of psychotherapy," Masson offers little in the way of new approaches to the helping relationship:

I have some ideas about how people could live without psychotherapy or psychiatry. I am thinking of self-help groups that are leaderless and avoid authoritarian structures, in which no money is exchanged, that are not grounded on religious principles (a difficulty with Alcoholics Anonymous and similar groups, since not all members share spiritual or religious interests), and in which all participants have experienced the problems they come to discuss. . . . What we need are more kindly friends and fewer professionals.

While I do not deny the usefulness of peer and support groups—or that "more kindly friends" are always good to find—I think it's obvious that this is no solution to the constant and growing need for psychological counseling. What we really need are more professionals who can genuinely help people undertake and accelerate the process of change in their lives. We humans have infinite resources, and therefore much to learn and teach about personal change and growth. Yet there already exist some workable approaches and practical techniques. In the next chapter, you will see how they can be applied in a guided self-change session.

CHAPTER 5:

Inside the Guided
Self-Change Session

Fortunately, analysis is not the only way to resolve inner conflicts. Life itself remains a very effective therapist.
—Karen Horney

After his first three sessions of guided self-change, a new client revealed to me what he was telling his friends about his "therapy": "I've told them that we have yet to meet in your office; that we just sit down and talk for two to three hours like normal people, except a lot more honestly; that if I ask you a question, you answer it; and that you ask questions and make suggestions for me to consider, but basically you go along with whatever I think is right to do. People say they've never heard of therapy like that!"

My reaction to this report: Isn't that *amazing*?! It's simply amazing to me that psychotherapy is generally expected to be a highly stylized, artificial form of human relationship—especially when its intent is to help people find their way to authentic relationships, improved self-esteem, and a renewed sense of purpose. Good relationships require that people be genuine with each other, and so you would naturally expect genuineness to be *modelled* in the relationship that's supposed to help you with all other relationships. The helping relationship is bound to be extraordinary, of course. But it doesn't have to be stilted and unreal.

I think most people come to therapy actually *wanting their lives to change*—even if they don't want to face the necessity of changing themselves—and pretty soon they find out that working on change is not the top priority of most therapists. They're more likely to find themselves under a therapist's scrutiny, as they're analyzed according to his particular theory of psychological reality. The therapist's dedication to applying that theoretical model virtually guarantees that an artificial process is going to be the norm, bearing no resemblance to an authentic relationship. The therapist will be reluctant to reveal his biases, knowledge, and inferences up front. In spite of his good intentions, the conventional therapist is like a poker player who's marked all the cards before you've entered the room. He's supposed to help you win the game, but that doesn't mean he'll let you see how the deck is stacked.

As a consultant paid to assist you in your self-change enterprise, I am not interested in taking care of you, staying ahead of you, or coming up with an elegant diagnosis of your problems. I assume you want some expert help in changing your life for the better. Since that's an enormous task, there's no sense in wasting time before getting down to it. The process of guided self-change is focused less on how you got to be the way you are, than on how you can attain a way of living every day in which you are true to yourself, caring to yourself and others, and accomplished at obtaining care and respect from others.

More Than A Change In Attitude

Although the styles of individual self-change consultants will vary as much as those of psychotherapists, I've synthesized some basic ideas, methods and techniques that I feel are indispensable to the process of guided self-change. They add up to much more than a modification of the therapeutic attitude. To those who have experienced psychotherapy, these changes in style, setting, and expectation may seem startling. To those who have never entered therapy, the basics of guided self-change may seem reasonable and quite natural—what you might expect of a professional but caring relationship devoted to the betterment of your life. I'll let you decide what that says about the current state of therapy.

The significance of each of these features will be discussed in more detail in this and later chapters. But as a means of introduction to the substantial differences between guided self-change and conventional psychotherapy, here they are in brief outline:

- *The guide's explicit endorsement of the values of respect, understanding, caring, and fairness*—and the client's endorsement by contractual agreement;

- *The use of tape recordings of all sessions*—for review and possession by the client, not the guide;

- *Self-disclosure and active participation on the part of the guide,* whose role is much more like that of a coach than a doctor;

- *Flexibility in meeting structure,* including the freedom to use non-office environments and 90-minute or longer sessions;

- *Discouragement of frequent consultations* in favor of frequent "homework": behavior and attitude experiments carried out by the client in everyday life between sessions;

- *Use of a practical, action-oriented counseling model expressed in everyday language* that is equally accessible to clients and consultants—in contrast to abstract, theoretical models expressed in arcane language used primarily by therapists discussing their cases out of their patients' earshot; and

- *Expectation that the client will eventually establish contact with her "inner spirit,"* the part of everyone that can provide a permanent, reliable, and uniquely personal sense of direction for growth.

Getting Underway

As you'll see in Chapter 6, "Helping Your Therapist Change," you can be involved in helping the *medical* model of psychotherapy evolve toward the *educational* model of guided self-change. If you want to experience guided self-change, you may have to help your current counselor learn about it, because there are presently very few guides using the complete model for change presented in this book. However, many counselors use some guided self-change principles, and the current healthy trend toward a "democratization" of therapy will make more of them increasingly accessible.

What follows is a description of how I conduct an initial guided self-change session. This book is not intended as an advertisement for my services, because I have more than enough to do. Indeed, I want to encourage established therapists to shift their orientation toward guided self-change—because I'd like to be able to send the many people who call and write me to counselors who use a self-change coaching process in lieu of therapy. But I hope this play-by-play description will help you (and your counselor) see how the seven principles of guided self-change are specifically applied in a typical session. If you've ever been in therapy, you will also detect some distinct differences in the kind of relationship I like to establish with my clients. (I have the funny idea that a professional counselor shouldn't hide his humanity from his clientele.)

You'd be getting accustomed to the challenges of guided self-change even before we met for our first full session, because you would have filled out my lengthy and infamous personal questionnaire, as well as a client worksheet and three-part consultation agreement (see the Appendix for models of these forms). At the end of the questionnaire, you'd give yourself a score on how well you were presently taking care of yourself. We'd both use this as a baseline from which to consider possible changes in your life. But a self-change guide would not review any such assessment questionnaire privately with the intent of drawing any diagnostic conclusions that were to be kept from you, even temporarily.

Regardless of what kind of preliminary test or inquiry a self-change consultant uses, the assessment of a client's starting point must be mutually candid. Otherwise, the ensuing relationship will be contaminated by some degree of manipulation, however well-intended.

Candor on the part of the guide is, in fact, crucial to the success of guided self-change at every stage. Dedication to candor avoids the generally well-intended but nonetheless disrespectful and demeaning tactics of most therapists, who feel they must weigh the possible impact of their honest observations against the vulnerabilities of their "impaired" patients. But candor need not be brutal. The helpfulness of a self-change guide will be determined by her proficiency in the "art of candor"—and the client's periodic review of the guide's artistry will be to both their benefits.

Now the first session would begin. My opening speech goes something like this:

"I see from the papers you filled out that you have [or haven't] had previous experience with counseling. You will find that I am an active participant in these sessions. As I see it, my job is to coach your efforts at improving your life. I am not your therapist, who is somehow going to make you better by using some technique in our sessions. The idea is to work together to analyze what's been going on in your life—your beliefs, attitudes, feelings, and actions. Then we can brainstorm and rehearse some experiments you can try in your daily life in order to find more satisfying ways of living. We want to accomplish this as efficiently as possible in terms of our time and your money. These sessions will help you prepare for your experiments, but it's your own courage in pursuing them outside our sessions that will change your life for the better—not the sessions themselves.

"As my secretary explained to you when you first called, we will tape-record this session so you can review it by yourself as soon as possible afterwards, at least within the next forty-eight hours. This tape is for your review only. I recommend against anyone else listening to it. In my experience, clients who diligently listen to the tapes of their sessions, and make notes about their thoughts and feelings, almost invariably change their lives in constructive ways, while those who don't review the tapes often gain very little from seeing me.

"It may surprise you to learn that the 'you' who listens and perhaps writes notes on your reactions to the tapes is more intelligent and ultimately more caring about yourself than the 'you' who is here talking with me today. You might say that I'm really talking to the 'self-observer' within your mind, who's going to become an increasingly important ally as our process goes on. The tape recording is literally an invitation to your self-observer to help us out.

"Do you have any questions about what we'll be doing here—or about me? Please don't hesitate to put me on the spot. We're going to be discussing highly personal issues in your life. You have a right to know with whom you're talking about these things. I'm prepared to tell you about my values, my own experience with personal change efforts, or anything you need to know about my approach to helping clients. You will find that I'm quite open about my own life experience, when it seems relevant to whatever you're working on.''

After any discussion inspired by this little speech, what would usually follow is a discussion of the value system that my clients have contractually agreed to honor as the basis of their self-change work. While most people find nothing offensive or objectionable to these values at an intellectual level —indeed, they strike most everyone as common sense—not many clients immediately comprehend what real commitment to these values may entail. My unabashed dedication to respect, understanding, caring, and fairness can be quite disconcerting for some.

Suppose a woman has come to me complaining bitterly of her husband's chronic lack of consideration for her, her children's disrespect, her employer's refusal to recognize her worth. Before long I am reacting viscerally to my new client's tales of abuse, and I ask:

''Are you telling me that your husband, boss, and children often talk to you that way?''

''They sure do,'' she sniffles.

''My God, that must feel awful,'' I say with genuine understanding and caring for her vulnerability. I'm beginning to be aware, however, that the woman's demeanor suggests that she habitually

seeks sympathy for her situation, in lieu of confronting her likely complicity in it.

"Yes," she adds weakly, "it feels absolutely
awful." At this stage, I'm conscious that our dialogue is already treading on the borderline of co-
dependency, where the client is all too ready to
incorporate me as merely a consoling ally in her
career of victimization. Yet my reaction will *not* be
a calculated tactic based on a therapeutic strategy of
discouraging co-dependency (or *encouraging* it, for
supposedly therapeutic reasons). I am going to
speak from my sense of dismay at the violation of
the values that I strive to model and uphold in my
own life. I will say something like this: "Please, can
you help me understand why you put up with these
painful attacks on your self-respect? Why have
you endured this for so long? I don't think I could
stand it."

With this kind of response—which may be more
or less confrontive depending on the particular
situation—I've put my client on notice that I find
self-abuse, whether active or passive, intolerable. I
always make it clear that I can't be paid enough to
witness masochism for very long without encouraging the client to take better care of herself. Why
should anyone tolerate painful treatment that erodes
self-respect? Why ignore the spirit's cries for help?

Suppose, then, that my new client responds that
she knows she should stand up for herself, but
doesn't know how. "I know I let everyone run all
over me," she confesses, "but I just haven't got
what it takes to do what I know I should do."

Now the opportunity has arisen for the discussion

of *courage*, the engine that really drives the process of change. The courage to change begins with the willingness to look at your life in a new way, which psychotherapy would encourage. But psychotherapy often takes people no further than the stage of new insights into their continuing dysfunction and unhappiness. Insight is only a tool that can be used in the process of change. You must still integrate your insights into your daily behavior and relationships, and that requires experimentation. It's the job of the self-change consultant to coach it.

Part of the difficulty in trying out new ways of being is that people instinctively know they may discover new and very frightening feelings. What is usually less obvious to people at first is that they may encounter a greater sense of their own power —and that's frightening, too.

Almost everyone I've coached to take a respectful but more assertive stance with a boss or spouse, for instance, has found that the person they've been having trouble with backs down and begins to relate with greater fairness. Yet for many people, eliciting that desired response doesn't lead to an increased likelihood of repeating the assertive behavior— which the psychology of conditioning would predict.

One reason for this is that you can't repeat such a new, successful behavior without realizing that your whole life up to that point was much more in your control than you've always thought. Some people don't want to face the fact that their sense of well-being is much more determined by their own attitudes and actions than by the external factors they blame or credit. And so, changing yourself entails *the risk of accepting responsibility for your own destiny*.

By its deliberate coaching of self-respect and courage, guided self-change is the most likely approach to move anyone toward the acceptance of that responsibility. Therapy too often encourages people to talk endlessly about their problems, their weaknesses, and their failures—while session after expensive session goes by. Later in this chapter, I'll discuss fully my reasons for steadily *decreasing* the frequency of sessions with my clients. Briefly put, I regard the increasing autonomy of clients as evidence of my effectiveness and, more importantly, the growth of their courage.

I don't believe that we should spend countless months analyzing problems in the hope that insight and catharsis will someday lead to the desired changes in my clients' lives. I think we can be working on real change right away. That's why the discussion of courage—a potential that everyone has to some degree—will come fairly early in the self-change process.

To maximize the potential of that discussion, however, we need to include an invisible but indispensable partner: the client's own self-observer.

Invitation to the Self-Observer: The Tape

Everyone has the capacity for self-observation. In fact, the ability to be aware of what we're doing, and the context in which we are doing it, is the aspect of consciousness that distinguishes the human being from all other animals. (I wouldn't be surprised to learn that porpoises and whales are self-observers too, but we don't know for sure.) In self-change sessions, I've found that the best way to enhance the natural self-observing capacity of clients is to tape-record our meetings, immediately giving the tapes to clients for their review as soon as possible after each session.

My opening speech introduces the self-observer as the "you" who is more intelligent, compassionate, and caring than the "you" who shows up in my office. People who have decided to seek out any form of therapy are often intimately identified with their pain. The self-observer is the mind's eye with an overview of an individual's total experience—and it has usually been exiled from awareness to some extent. By handing the client the tape of our conversation at the end of our meeting, I'm explicitly inviting the self-observer to return and work with us.

That may not always happen right away. One client of mine faithfully saved his tapes, but avoided listening to them until after he had graduated from an alcohol addiction rehabilitation program I had repeatedly recommended. Thereafter he wrote me to say that he had been able to appreciate and learn from his tapes only since he had achieved sobriety. In essence, his self-observer had been sedated and unavailable while our sessions were taking place.

What does taping achieve? First of all, it shifts the emphasis from what happens in the consultation session to what the client does afterward, beginning with review of the tape. I strongly recommend to clients that they make journal notes about what comes up in their reactions to the tapes: powerful feelings, new ideas, disagreements with anything I said, hunches about what we should pursue next.

It's important that the client has a chance to review *me*. Because of the relative vulnerability of anyone who comes to a professional seeking help in their lives, there's a tendency to suspend skepticism about what that professional says. But in review and reflection, a client may be able to spot sophistry, illogic, or other inaccuracies in a guide's remarks which seemed brilliant in the emotionally charged atmosphere of a session.

Hence, the tape also shifts the emphasis away from the professional's authority and toward equality between client and coach, which is as it should be. Not incidentally, this suggests a greater legal vulnerability on the part of the self-change guide, compared to that of a therapist who keeps the only record of sessions in the form of notes. I've had lawyer-clients ask me in amazement, "Are you kidding? You've giving everybody tapes of your sessions? What good are your notes of what happened if the client has the tapes?"

I reply that I never take notes during a session. I don't enjoy taking them, and I feel it makes an authentic dialogue difficult if not entirely impossible. I rarely make notes even after a session, although I believe that practice is much to be preferred to writing during sessions. I'm simply much more interested in where my clients are going than where they have been, and I'm not interested in having detailed records of anyone as a "case history."

This brings up another significant fact: with the

tape, *the client owns the history of the relationship with the guide.* In conventional therapy, the therapist is the only one who can reconstruct, and therefore interpret, what has gone before: "According to my notes, here is what you thought six months ago." By contrast, I encourage people to save their earliest tapes, and key ones thereafter (if not all of them), because the tapes can actually gain in usefulness as time goes on—as their self-observer becomes more alert, compassionate, and sophisticated.

When clients are feeling down because of an unhappy incident—or are still working on the key distinction between *feeling* bad and *being* bad—they may sometimes think they're losing ground. In that case I will often suggest, "If you think you're slipping, why don't you go back and listen to your first tape? You can compare how you sounded then with how you sound now. If you really think that you're back where you started, I'll refund all your money." Most people are tremendously reassured when they go back and hear the person who first came to see me, the person who was comparatively plaintive, evasive of personal responsibility, and lacking in self-respect.

Thus, the tapes also provide the client with an effective measure of the success of the work. It's not the fulfillment of theoretical predictions that counts in guided self-change, it's the client's own sense of personal growth and fulfillment. And with increased fulfillment comes an accelerated sense of understanding. A philosophy professor I've counseled has told me that he listens to his first two session tapes over and over again, because he missed so much when he was actually there and in his first review of the tapes. Only recently has his compassionate self-observer begun to participate—and as it does, the professor gets more and more out of his early sessions.

Therapists would probably argue that the taping of sessions is going to inhibit clients, but some therapists I've talked to have admitted that it would more likely be inhibiting to *them*. A review of psychiatric literature I've done indicates that not more than one in a thousand psychiatrists tapes sessions for the client's use. The only context in which recording is extensively used is in psychiatric training and research, and then the tapes are used only as a means of reviewing student therapists' performance or compiling research data.

Certainly, some clients are initially unwilling to tape. I tell them that I'm willing to have one session without taping, but I always implore them to reconsider before we begin. My speech on the matter goes like this:

"We'll never be able to recapture this session. The 'feeling tone,' the intensity, the newness, all of that will never happen again, even if we cover the same ground in later sessions. If we tape it and you don't want to listen to it, then you can destroy it as soon as the session's over. It's your tape, and the only one that will exist. I don't record for my use, and I'm not going to keep a copy. Do what you want with it. But I strongly urge you to let us tape this first session, and **then** decide what to do with it."

I also have clients sign a form stating my recommendation that they do not share their tapes with anyone else. I'll safekeep tapes for clients after they've reviewed them, if they feel that's absolutely necessary. But it's important that they feel no one else is or will be "listening in," even in their imagination. If clients really want to play a particular tape for a spouse or friend, I always recommend that they play it through completely one time alone, while imagining that the other person is there. That's the best way to make sure that they really want someone else to share it.

Further, I suggest that it would be far better to paraphrase what happened in a session than to play the tape for someone else. Playing a tape for someone else can set up a precedent that the client may not want to continue: "Why were you willing to play the last tape for me and not this one?" Also, relying on the tape to communicate to others about one's self-change work suggests that the client may not really be ready to talk about the subject at hand—as if he needs the tape to do the talking for him. (I tell clients the same thing about quoting me: "If you learn something in this session and you want to adopt it in your life, then it's yours. But if you just quote me, you lose your power. Telling your spouse or friends that 'Dr. Rusk said to do this or that' is a sure way to lose respect and credibility.")

It's interesting that some clients feel they cannot maintain the confidentiality of their own tapes. Some people will actually turn off the recorder during parts of a session when they want to talk about things they don't respect themselves for thinking, feeling, or doing: "I don't know, I just don't feel comfortable with this.'' So the taping creates a whole psychological dynamic of its own. It can make a person aware of what is difficult enough to hear herself say out loud, let alone have to listen to it again. This self-censorship presents another opportunity for the client to realize that the self-observer possesses a greater maturity than the everyday personality. As a person progresses along the path of change, her compassionate self-observer begins to replace her habitual, self-doubting personality.

By and large, most people are delighted by the idea of taping at the outset, and they can't understand why all therapists don't do it. After their first few reviews of their sessions, they're absolutely amazed that taping isn't standard practice—because they can see for themselves that comparatively little would happen without it. Clients of mine with previous experience in psychotherapy have confessed that they often told therapists what they thought therapists wanted to hear. Of course, the tape makes such behavior pointless. The self-change guide is there to help you learn and grow. The record of your work is for your study only.

This is one means by which I emphasize that there's no use in trying to please or manipulate me, because I don't look down on clients from a higher perch. I have my own share of struggles to keep my life in balance; I'm not interested in taking on responsibility for the lives of clients too. I'm a mentor, not a boss or parent. In stating my limits and limitations clearly from the outset, I serve another indispensable principle of guided self-change: the authenticity of the helping relationship.

Transference vs. The Modeling of Healthy Communication

To put it simply, you can expect a self-change guide to be talking much more during a session than a psychotherapist would talk. The amount of dialogue between a guide and client is similar to what would occur between a lawyer or architect and their clients. Both kinds of professionals want to draw you out and hear what your needs are, while clearly establishing or fulfilling their roles and responsibilities for the contractual partnership. There's no reason for the self-change consultation to be substantially different in this respect. Whatever the problems of a client, I regard him as a whole person who is signing a contract for the specialized services of another whole person. The particular kind of help I'm providing is no cause for an artificial relationship.

This is a big change from the popular notion that a person in therapy pours out her feelings to someone who is fairly impassive, only grunting now and then or demonstrating a professionally restrained empathy for the duration of a fifty-minute hour. This classic therapeutic scenario derives from the Freudian idea that the therapist must serve as a kind of "blank screen" which ideally invites the patient's *transference*.

Transference is a scientific-sounding word that refers to the tendency to treat a therapist as if he were a parent or other significant person from the client's childhood. Transferring your oldest habitual patterns of relationship to the psychotherapist is supposed to allow him to provide you with the key

to understanding your inner world. This understanding of your history provides you with the cure
for what "ails" you. Then the therapist helps you
resolve these antiquated transferences with carefully
worded and timed interpretations.

In psychotherapeutic training a great deal is made
of the transference and how to use it to the greatest
advantage—which amounts to a behind-the-scenes
manipulation of the helping relationship by the therapist. Likewise, the consequences of the *countertransference*—the fact that a therapist will also tend to
develop positive and negative emotional reactions to
the patient—have been thoroughly dissected and
discussed in professional literature. At its best, all
this theorizing is grist for the academic mill. At its
worst, it enhances the mystification of therapy and
infantilizes those who come to seek help.

While I don't have much use for the words anymore, I can say that I hope for a positive, respectful, caring transference and countertransference. My
intent is to coach my clients to experiment, change,
and learn to care for themselves and others better.
Those are my standard goals. I do not expect clients
to help me with my life's challenges, which distinguishes our exchange from the intimate equality of
a nonprofessional friendship. I'm more honest, vulnerable, and self-disclosing than a typical psychotherapist, but I'm there to serve my clients;
they're not there to serve me.

My definition of the useful transference is the
metaphor of a coach, mentor, or trail guide. I'm like
a wilderness scout who tells you where to set up
camp and how to build a fire. But it's your expedition, and ultimately you make all the decisions

about how far and how fast to go. If you consistently ignore my advice and insist on courting unreasonable danger, I may bail out. I won't keep watching and listening to continuing attempts to self-destruct. It simply hurts me too much, and it encourages you to keep hurting yourself. I have terminated consulting relationships for this reason, more often than any therapists I know.

By contrast, the classic psychotherapeutic transference is almost inevitably dependent. Theoretically it is meant to *emerge*, and not be imposed by the therapist, and it nearly always emerges as a parental or authoritarian relationship. A therapist can usually tell when this process is beginning to take place, and generally does not remark to the client about the first signs of emergence.

Any time a client consciously or unconsciously attempts to construct a parental transference with me, however ("Do you think I should come back for another session?" "Should I separate from my wife?") I'm going to laugh out loud, or scream, or simply say, "Forget it! You aren't paying me enough to take this on. I have enough trouble running my own life. I'm not about to take on the responsibility of running yours, too!"

I'd much rather that clients regard me as a *model of healthy communication* than a surrogate parent. To be such a model, I simply have to be a human being who teaches and demonstrates what I've learned so far about self-management, communication, and relationships. I am identifying myself as an expert, but that doesn't mean I'm an authority who requires or deserves obedience.

What helps keeps that distinction clear is my willingness to reveal the fullness of my own humanity: my needs, feelings, mistakes, fears, and foibles. This means that I will share with clients experiences from my own life that have some bearing on the work they are doing in the self-change process. It's my experience that the more I disclose about myself and my struggle to live a value-driven life, the less likely I am to be mistaken for an omniscient authority or a parental figure.

The Importance of the Guide's Self-Disclosure

In a case history in *Love's Executioner*—which I recommend as a spellbinding account of psychotherapy at its best—Irvin D. Yalom illustrates the importance of self-disclosure while tellingly identifying it as a "therapeutic" technique. A patient he calls Marge, who had begun to exhibit a dramatic split between the passive and aggressive aspects of her personality, responded positively to Yalom's disclosures about his wife, whom Marge had envied. Marge later told her therapist:

> *"The main thing that turned me around—in fact, the moment the calm set in—was when you told me that your wife and I had similar problems at work. I feel I'm so icky, so creepy and your wife's so holy that we couldn't both be mentioned in the same breath. Confiding to me that she and I had some of the same problems **proved** you had some respect for me. . . . you've often **told** me you respected me, and told me you liked me, but it was just words. I never really believed it. This time it was different, you went beyond words."*

Actually Yalom did use "just words," but they were self-disclosing words. He comments:

> Going "beyond words," **that** was what counted. It was what I **did**, not what I said. It was actually **doing** something for the patient. Sharing something about my wife was doing something for Marge, giving her a gift. **The therapeutic act, not the therapeutic word.**

I think Yalom's self-disclosure to Marge helped her precisely because it was not a therapeutic act, but an *authentic* act of human communication. He never really went beyond words. But he did go beyond the "blank screen," the transference, and all the other artificial boundaries of communication that the medical model of psychotherapy imposes. Marge herself understood this, for she told Yalom:

> "Also, it helped that you didn't get into your role of the wizard letting me guess about questions you know the answers to. I liked the way you admitted you didn't know and then invited me to explore it together with you."

"Music to my ears!" exclaims Yalom, adding this revealing comment:

> Throughout my year of work with Marge, I had only a single real rule in my work—treat her as an equal.

That rule makes sense to me, too. In fact, I stopped practicing conventional psychotherapy so that I would be able to follow it consistently in my personal and professional life.

One last note from Marge's case history. Yalom reports that by the end of their work together,

Marge had begun to integrate the two wildly divergent aspects of her personality, and had become more genuine and straightforward as a result. As her self-respect grew, she began to think of her therapist as a human being like herself:

> For the first time, she began asking me personal questions. "How did you decide to get into this field? Have you ever regretted it? Do you ever get bored? With me? What you do with your problems?" Marge had appropriated the bold parts of the other Marge as I urged her to do, and it was important that I be receptive and respectful to each of her questions.

Yes indeed! Why should it ever be otherwise? When a human being asks you questions in an intimate setting, where you're supposed to be helping her change her ways of living and believing— with all due respect, what else do you have any right to do?

What many therapists do is "turn back" such questions on their clients, asking something like, "Why are you so interested in my life?" In most cases, I regard this as an inauthentic and useless ploy therapists use to hide from their patients and defend their own sense of authority and superiority. Since I offer my openness in my introductory speech to clients, it's not unusual for them to ask me how I got into my line of work in the very first session, and in most cases I answer them immediately. Anyone who has experienced psychotherapy as a patient will appreciate that this openness is a revolutionary departure from standard practice— and a return to simple human communication.

Now if I sense that such a question is being pur-

sued as a diversion from the real task at hand—
helping the client approach the process of self-
change—I will instead promise to answer the inquiry
later in the session, and then ask, "Would you allow me to postpone my answer for now, and help
me understand why that's important to you at this
moment?" I will then explain that I want to use the
energy behind the question for the purpose of our
meeting: to help the client change her life. If I
momentarily postpone answering any question
directed to me, I will always explain *why* I'm doing
so; clients have a right to that explanation. But I always keep my promise to respond.

Another way in which I discourage a dependent
transference is by setting clear limits on my availa-
bility for consultation. Generally speaking, I am not
"on call" for emergencies in the sense that many
medical doctors are, and my personal preference is
to be somewhat difficult to contact outside the meeting sessions. I try to make it clear to clients that
I'd much rather give up my privacy through self-
disclosure *during* sessions than sacrifice my private
life *outside* sessions.

I am not suggesting that my extreme degree of
unavailability is fundamental to the guided self-
change process. A guide's degree of accessibility
outside sessions will vary according to her individual preference; every professional has the right
to determine how much of herself and her life's time
she is willing to offer her clients. The point is to help
clients develop a sense of mutual respect and
balance in relationship to the guide—even during
moments of crisis—so that they can gradually learn
to keep their center when the going gets tough, and

not expect a professional rescuer to be immediately available every time. It's important to recognize that the guide, like the client, is also a needy and vulnerable human being, not an all-powerful and immediately available caretaker.

That's why, with rare exceptions, I do not see people more than once a week even at the inception of our relationship, and I encourage them to meet with me less frequently after the first three or four encounters. On the other hand, I often use sessions of ninety minutes or longer (two hours minimum for couples), and I'm open to meeting with clients in nonprofessional environments, including their home or mine. (In home environments, I generally make certain that someone else is nearby but out of earshot of our session, to discourage any seductive overtones. And, as always, sessions are tape-recorded for the client's benefit.) All of these considerations serve to keep self-change sessions in the realm of person-to-person conversations, rather than doctor-to-patient treatments.

I discourage frequent meetings not just to save time and clients money—which are important considerations—but chiefly because of my stated philosophy that what happens *between* our sessions is more important than what happens during them. In our meetings, I'm providing support, encouragement, a little collaborative analysis, and a lot of assistance in brainstorming and rehearsing self-change experiments that clients must then carry out in the "real world," without my presence. The real world is where clients' problems first arose, and that's where they must be solved—by trying out new ideas and approaches to life.

From Psychodrama to Homework

The emphasis on real-world experimentation is another dramatic departure from the psychotherapeutic model, which regards the "psychodrama" that goes on in the therapy session as a kind of medicine administered to the patient. That medicine —whose quality depends largely on the expertise and personality of the therapist—is supposed to result in healing insight and catharsis.

It's a tremendous expectation to think you can have an effective psychodrama within a particular fifty minutes by appointment—which is why therapists end up seeing some clients four or five times a week. Another cause of frequent sessions is that psychoanalytically-oriented therapy tends to treat the *problems* of people with more interest and respect than it does their *potentials*. The pathological bias of medicine makes this kind of "treatment" inevitable.

Unfortunately, that pathological bias also tends to reinforce a troubled person's beliefs in his own weakness and inadequacy. Without knowing that there could be other, more fruitful ways to address his problems, he buys into the notion that he must accept the patient role and be treated by a medical or paramedical professional. While awaiting insight and catharsis, the "patient" is encouraged not to make major decisions about the conduct of his life.

By contrast, I'm encouraging my clients to make conscious, value-driven decisions at every possible moment, or else we're going nowhere. Guided self-change proposes that the distressed and dissatisfied person will respond best to experiential education and encouragement, not treatment. In the original Latin (*educere*), education means "to draw out." As a coach of change, I am intent on drawing out the compassionate self-observer and inner spirit of my clients. The best way to strengthen those aspects of consciousness is through real-world experiments in attitude and behavior, the "homework" of guided self-change.

Advocacy for the Client's Spirit

My primary focus is on what heals clients, not what ails them. What heals clients is their own authenticity: the ability to self-observe, the courage to act on their inner sense of right and wrong, a deep capacity for love, and the human birthright of respect, understanding, caring, and fairness. This value system is not an airy philosophical construction; it's a common-sense blueprint for mental health, emotional happiness, and creative productivity.

At the level of our original innocence, we all know these things. What's popularly called our "inner child" is often found to be wounded precisely because our deep, authentic values have been attacked and laid to siege. The first attacks may have been beyond our control, happening to us when we were children ourselves. They may not even have been intentional on the part of the perpetrators. Yet at some point, in defensive response to our wounds and pain, we all adopt these vengeful, nihilistic behaviors as part of our adult personality—while seldom taking full adult responsibility for healing ourselves with the kind of respect and caring of which we were deprived.

Because most of us live the lives of such "habitual" selves, it's no surprise that the route to a more authentic way of living involves the confrontation and reevaluation of our familiar ways of being. The expertise of a self-change guide lies partly in the fact that he is almost invariably more capable of recognizing the beauty and vulnerability of a client's authentic self than the client himself.

The inner self regularly needs to be heard, and many of our mental, emotional, and bodily dysfunctions are in fact its distorted expressions. But the inner self has no administrative, decision-making capacities. It is dependent on the alertness and sensitivity of the daily operating self for its messages to be deciphered and acted upon. It's the operating self that I'm coaching; it's the inner self that I'm asking my clients to join me in listening to and calling upon, all the while encouraging clients to take over my role and outgrow as rapidly as possible the need for my assistance.

To recognize and stimulate the client's capacity for authentic relationship, courageous risk-taking and creative growth is to be an advocate for the client's spirit. That's the most direct path to "soul healing," the noble goal which psychotherapy was originally intended to accomplish.

CHAPTER 6:

"Teach Me, Don't Treat Me": Helping Your Therapist Change

He was meddling too much in my private life.
—Tennessee Williams,
explaining why he stopped
seeing his psychoanalyst

Imagine that you are entering therapy for the first time. You've been referred to a reputable psychotherapist and now you're sitting in his office. After introductions have been exchanged, it's time for you to state your reasons for seeking professional help. You might say something like this:

"I'm having a lot of troubles in my life. I just don't know what's wrong. I feel depressed and afraid all the time, and I can't focus on anything. I probably have some kind of mental disorder. I hope you can find out what it is and cure me. Do you think that will take a long time?"

But you could say something like this:

"I'm having a lot of troubles in my life. I'm not sure what's wrong, but I'm tense and depressed and so I know I must be off the track somehow. I'm looking for someone who can help me learn to take better care of myself. I don't want to waste time or money, so I hope we can get right down to work. I'm ready to change, but I need some guidance.''

Unusual as it may seem, you have every right to take the latter approach—and you owe it to yourself. By summoning the courage to seek professional help for psychological difficulties, you have already undertaken a significant experiment in self-change. You deserve not to be slowed down in your process, and you deserve experienced, caring guidance expressed in plain language. You certainly don't need to presume that you are ill or defective—or to be treated as if you are—and you don't need anyone to pretend that he can cure you. You may be seriously troubled, but you can still specify the kind of help you prefer.

If you'd rather be coached and educated than treated, then you are opting for the model of guided self-change as described in this book. Unfortunately, the field of guided self-change consultation does not exist as yet, although there are some progressive therapists who use some of its principles. Currently your best opportunity for obtaining skillful and informed private guidance with the self-change process is to convince an experienced, qualified therapist to shift from his standard approach and adopt a non-medical guidance mode in your case.

The current state of counseling and psychotherapy makes this idea less far-fetched than it may first appear. To begin with, there is the matter of supply and demand. So many people have entered the field of counseling and psychotherapy over the past two decades that it is a buyers' market in most urban areas. ''Consumers'' of therapy have far greater leverage than ever before in contracting for exactly the kind of counseling they want.

Secondly, it would be a mistake to assume that a therapist will be offended by a potential client's announcement of the desire to help define the nature of their professional relationship. In fact, most therapists would be astounded at their good fortune in having such a highly motivated prospective client appear. They would probably check to make certain they weren't dreaming, or the subject of a fellow therapist's practical joke. Thus, you could be confident that you are doing the therapist a favor by entering his office willing to change your attitudes and behavior, and offering some specific ideas about how you can be effectively helped. The difficulty lies in being clear and concise about your needs and intent at a time when many of your thoughts and feelings may be in turmoil and distress.

Writing Your Manifesto

You can take a giant step forward in your self-change process by writing out an explicit description of the kind of counseling you want before you enter a therapist's office. Writing such a manifesto will help you begin developing a self-observant capacity, as you will be forced to think less about your specific problems than about the best way to develop solutions for them all.

The ''Self-Change Manifesto'' that follows is a model you can use to craft your own personal statement about how you'd like to approach the process of self-change and the professional helping relationship. I recommend that you copy it for your own use and make whatever changes that seem appropriate to your needs. For instance, you might want to specify that you'd like to pursue dream interpretation as an aspect of your self-change process. While guided self-change does not focus on such analytic techniques, it certainly doesn't preclude their use. (For a fuller discussion of this issue, see Chapter 7, "When Is Therapy Appropriate?") No specific techniques are written into this model manifesto, so that it will be adaptable to as many readers as possible. However, the broad principles of the guided self-change approach are all included, and I recommend that you think over each one carefully in drafting your personal manifesto.

Your finished version should be as dramatic and challenging as you can make it, for it will serve as your own "declaration of independence"—not only from any sense of helplessness you may have developed, but also from ineffective, co-dependent modes of treatment you might otherwise be subjected to as a passive "patient" of psychotherapy. Your manifesto will also serve as a landmark for the beginning of your self-change process—something you can look back on with well-deserved pride as your personal growth progresses.

THE SELF-CHANGE MANIFESTO

For the Reader Seeking Expert Help

I want to change my life. If I hope to change for the better, I realize I must develop new attitudes, new behavior, even new beliefs—especially about myself. But I know that self-change is difficult. I can use intelligent, informed and caring support from an expert who will help me stand back from myself, identify my full range of options, and then devise self-change experiments that move me in the direction of my goals.

I expect a personal change expert to help me discover and make better use of my innate talents; to help me better understand and manage myself and my feelings; to help me treat myself and others with greater respect, understanding, caring, and fairness; and to help me make certain I am treated well in return.

I see myself as a highly motivated student of guided self-change. I am eager to explore new and unfamiliar ways of thinking and acting, despite any awkwardness and discomfort I may feel along the way. If there is good reason to believe that I might also benefit from medication or some other treatment procedure, I may be willing to try that option—once I have carefully reviewed all the potential risks and benefits.

What I don't want from my personal change consultant is to be treated as if I am impaired or defective, a patient who is ill and requires therapy in order to be fixed. In other words: *Teach me, don't treat me.*

If I choose you as my consultant, I will look to you as a model to inspire me by practicing what you preach. I assume that you have had significant success changing your own life and that you continue to challenge yourself to keep growing. I would appreciate hearing about some of your self-initiated changes and how you accomplished them, at least insofar as your experiences are relevant to my life and goals for change.

In brief, I am looking for a gifted, enthusiastic personal change coach, who will teach, confront, and encourage me— an expert counselor deserving of my trust, a guiding partner in my self-change efforts.

What Kind of Person Should You Seek as a Guide?

Keep in mind that therapists are not simply average people who randomly selected their line of work from a number of equally profitable choices. Like specialists in any field, many therapists self-select because of their inborn abilities and for their own special needs and motivations, both conscious and unconscious. It is now known that therapists and psychiatrists generally have certain characteristic vulnerabilities and motivations. As Thomas Maeder, himself a child of two therapists, wrote in his book *Children of Psychiatrists and Other Psychotherapists*:

> *In speaking to the children of psychotherapists, I have been forcibly struck by the number that bring up their parents' emotionally dismal childhoods. They paint portraits of their therapist-parents as exceptionally lonely and unhappy, socially ostracized at school and abused at home, either psychologically or, sometimes, physically. They were people who had been ill at ease with themselves and with others, who sought through association with the world of adults and a retreat into the world of the intellect, and ultimately through the field of psychotherapy to understand and manage their misery and to protect themselves and, later, their families. In many cases the parents themselves had invoked their unhappy early lives as the primary motivation for their ultimate career choice, while in others the story seemed sufficiently clear that the children drew their conclusion on their own. These children usually love their parents, and almost invariably admire them, yet quite often, there is also the sense of something a little pathetic about it all, something sad and vulnerable and in need of protection.*

Both the best and the worst of therapists are usually people who have experienced emotional wounding and insufficient understanding or comforting during childhood. As a result, they grew up with significant doubts about themselves and their intrinsic worth. Depending on a particular therapist's degree of dedication to responsible self-change, this traumatic background can serve either positive or negative purposes. On the one hand, it can assist the therapist by providing a sophisticated empathy for others' suffering. On the other, it can create distancing and a tendency to manipulate and control patients in order to compensate for the therapist's own childhood hurts.

The number and impressiveness of the diplomas on a therapist's wall will not tell you whether he is empathetic or manipulative, or somewhere in between. From a conventional perspective, one has little to go on besides academic credentials and professional reputation in assessing a therapist's effectiveness. He is the one who is supposed to apply sophisticated psychological techniques to a passive patient who has neither the specialized education nor (it is assumed) the common-sense capacity to assess whether those techniques are appropriate and effectively administered. A patient's objections to a certain course of treatment may be interpreted as resistance or a "need to control"—both seen as indications of pathology—and inquiries about the therapist's own experience (with the kind of issues that concern the patient) will be regarded as inappropriate and unhealthy.

In your search for an effective self-change guide, you might not go far wrong by simply turning all these therapeutic standards inside-out. An MFCC (Marriage and Family Counselor) is likely to be more flexible and less dogmatic than a psychiatric MD or institute-certified psychoanalyst (although you shouldn't automatically hold anyone's degrees against him). You certainly don't want to pay good money to anyone who will not fully explain his ideas and approaches in down-to-earth language. Your right to help determine the style of your counseling should be enthusiastically embraced by a prospective self-change guide. And finally, a counselor who rigidly refuses any self-disclosure should be regarded with some suspicion.

The five points below can serve as a general guideline for what you *do* want in a self-change guide. Note that none of these capacities are defined or precluded by modern psychological training. However, they are the kind of credentials more likely earned in the "school of life" by someone who has keenly experienced the need to change her way of being, and courageously undertaken the experiments necessary to bring about change. Thus, the kind of person you should seek as a self-change guide is:

- *Someone who has made deliberate, positive changes in her own life and sees herself as someone actively pursuing personal growth, with or without outside help;*

- *Someone who is sufficiently secure about himself that he would be willing to risk some changes in his professional approach, at least in your case;*

- *Someone who is willing to admit her vulnerabilities, limitations, and mistakes, but who accepts and affirms her self-worth;*

- *Someone who is enthusiastic about working with a person as motivated and responsible as you are;*

- *Someone who seeks out and accepts comforting for his own pain, and is willing to reveal how he has learned to do that as part of your self-change education.*

Negotiating a Trial Period of Guided Self-Change

Because therapists are generally sensitive and wounded folks—and because they have to be highly intelligent to succeed in their postgraduate studies —it pays to be gentle and diplomatic in negotiating for self-change guidance instead of therapy. It's always easier to negotiate what you want before you begin, so let's address how you might approach a therapist who has been recommended to you by a satisfied client as being caring and open (the best form of referral).

Explain that you are interested in meeting him in person for just fifteen to twenty minutes—at no charge to you—to see if you seem compatible. Emphasize that you are ambitious about changing, and willing to work hard at it. If a therapist refuses this type of preliminary interview, then he is unlikely to be flexible enough to consider your unusual request for a new mode of professional counseling.

You can begin the meeting by briefly explaining what you want—in terms of the broad principles of guided self-change—with or without a personal manifesto in hand. Then give the therapist every chance to explain any reservations he may have about what you are proposing. Don't argue. Quite the contrary, you want to elicit his complete position on the issue, and then repeat it back to him considerately and respectfully in your own words. Then check to be certain that he feels you have grasped his point of view accurately.

Only after this debriefing of your prospective guide is complete should you explain in detail your reasons for wanting guided self-change instead of therapy. Ask the therapist to take your proposition under advisement and consider granting it for a trial period of two to three months. Should either of you be dissatisfied after that time, you would be willing to consider shifting to a more traditional approach. Leave the therapist a copy of this book, and tell him to call me if he wishes to ask any questions about the approach.

Explain further that you would be willing to take full responsibility for this experiment in guided self-change, and that you will give the therapist a written statement absolving him of responsibility for any lack of progress or any ill effects that might ensue during the trial period. The statement should document that you are not retaining his services as a therapist, but as a consultant or advisor to your own self-change efforts. In other words, you are explicitly refusing a doctor-patient or therapist-client relationship.

After the trial period, this statement could be renewed for the duration of your counseling. This should help ease any anxiety your therapist has about taking on an innovative approach, since you are essentially relieving him of standard therapeutic responsibilities. A self-change guide is there to help you devise and carry out experiments for improving your life, but you must be ultimately responsible for their failure or success. Anyone contemplating the pursuit of guided self-change must therefore consider an important question: Are you willing to assume full responsibility for your own process of personal growth?

Another responsibility issue arises when you let the guide know that you would not necessarily expect him to be on emergency call, since he is not your therapist in the usual sense. Some people may find this unavailability unsettling, and may instead want to negotiate a limited access to their guide outside appointed sessions, in agreement with the preference of the guide. But it is important to remember that when you propose guided self-change as a model for the counseling of your personal growth, you are dispensing with the idea of a psychological supervisor who's supposed to come to your emotional rescue when the going gets tough.

If the need for a rescuer is a potent issue for you at the onset of counseling, you should discuss with your guide the widest possible network of resources you can construct that may serve the same purpose: support groups, peer counselors, close friends, etc. Focusing all your expectations for emergency psychological assistance on one person, regardless of who it is, constitutes an unhealthy transfer of personal responsibility.

In guided self-change, the alternative is to accept responsibility for finding the help you need at intense moments, and doing so in a manner that is fair and respectful to both yourself and others. This is better done by having a variety of responses to extreme duress at your disposal—possibly including meditation, self-hypnosis, deep breathing techniques, vigorous exercise, therapeutic artwork, and so on—to supplement any talking-through you may need from friends or advisors.

You and your guide may agree on mutually respectful guidelines for emergency consultations, but I personally believe that such consultations should be rare in guided self-change. In my experience, there are very few people who are not capable of this degree of self-reliance. In fact, it usually sounds less daunting to people who are first-time clients than to those who are accustomed to psychotherapists acting as rescuers.

These and other ramifications of guided self-change may bring up the question of whether health insurance should properly cover a counseling approach which is educational rather than medical. For the time being, you and the therapist may come to an understanding with your guide that your counseling will still be referred to as therapy for the purposes of payment by health insurance. A diagnosis is generally required for insurance purposes; you can explicitly discuss and negotiate your diagnosis with your guide. In general, I suggest choosing "Adjustment Disorder," which has less likelihood of harming your reputation than more serious diagnoses such as "Depression."

In a future that would see conventional therapy largely replaced by various educational approaches, it is conceivable that the burden of payment would be shifted to employers who would invest profitably in the rapid psychological growth and ethical development of employees pursuing guided self-change as part of their employee assistance programs. It's important to note that guided self-change requires far fewer sessions between client and counselor, and therefore considerably less expense, than the traditional therapeutic mode. The full range of potential legal and financial implications of replac-

ing psychotherapy with guided self-change is beyond the scope of this book, but I look forward to
addressing them more fully as the concept becomes
more widely accepted.

What Are the Major Changes You Are Requesting?

It will be helpful to make clear to a potential counselor the major alterations of the therapeutic approach that guided self-change requires. You can do
this either by handing him this book, or writing up
your own adaptation of the five requirements discussed below.

Five Requirements for
Guided Self-Change Counseling

1. *A strong focus in counseling sessions on learning
   to understand what your current feelings are saying to you;*

2. *More openness from your consultant about her
   ideas, feelings, opinions, observations, personal
   experiences, and values;*

3. *An agreement to tape-record all sessions for the
   exclusive possession and use of the client;*

4. *More brainstorming of new attitudes and actions
   for you to attempt between sessions; and*

5. *An agreement to regularly review your agenda for
   self-change.*

---

1. **A strong focus in counseling sessions on learning to understand what your current feelings are saying to you**—in relationship with yourself and others, and in light of the guiding values of respect, understanding, caring, and fairness. A potential guide must be willing to consider the perspective that feelings are messages from one's deep inner spirit (as discussed in detail in Chapter 2), and that learning to interpret them is the only sure way to recovering one's authentic equilibrium and natural creativity. While only the most mechanistic therapies would regard feelings as superfluous, even the most progressive therapies may fall short of giving feelings the primacy and spiritual significance they are afforded in guided self-change. You may have to allow a traditionally trained therapist some time to shift his emphasis and educate himself on this approach to feelings.

You may also discover that a scientifically-oriented therapist is unaccustomed to the discussion of the four basic values as a foundation for interpreting feelings. But he will be hard pressed to find a disadvantage in endorsing respect, understanding, caring, and fairness as guidelines to the process of psychological growth. Your role is not to enforce this or any other concept in the guidance relationship, but to bring such ideas up for early discussion and determine whether a practical agreement exists between you and the counselor on such fundamental issues.

2. **More openness from your consultant about her ideas, feelings, opinions, observations, personal experiences, and values**—in short, a substan-

tially higher degree of self-disclosure than is generally practiced in psychotherapy. However, it has to be clear that the guide's self-disclosure occurs at your request and bears a clear relationship to specific situations and issues that are going on with you. The point of the guide telling you about *her* life is *your* education—not the guide using your time to show off, complain, or sort out her problems. The educational purpose of guided self-change distinguishes appropriate self-disclosure from the intimate exchanges of a friendship or romance, which may chiefly serve the purposes of gossiping, commiseration, or seduction. (It should be clearly stated that a romantic liaison is no more appropriate or ethical in guided self-change than in therapy. The guide is hired to help you, not to use you to satisfy any needs for love, power, attention, admiration, or sexuality. What a guide can reasonably expect to receive for his services, besides payment, is the certain knowledge that he is performing a meaningful service to another human being.)

Because you are paying for an educational service, the entire focus of guided self-change sessions is on helping you work out your issues and learn to satisfy your needs *outside* sessions—through deliberate, courageous experiments in changing your attitudes and behavior—rather than *within* the session. Your encounters with the guide occur only to help you brainstorm those experiments and develop the skills needed to carry them out. In doing that, a talented and experienced guide will naturally have examples from her own life and from her observations of other people that are helpful to you.

As pointed out in the previous chapter, this kind

of self-disclosure helps keep a counselor human in a client's eyes, whereas the refusal of most therapists to talk about their experience tends to create images of them as bigger and purer than life. Therapists' relatively aloof stance also tends to exaggerate clients' feelings of inadequacy, since they reveal their neediness and vulnerability while therapists appear competent and problem-free. When a counselor is mistaken for a god, priest, or all-knowing expert, there is actually a much greater potential for abuse and co-dependency in the counseling relationship than there is with a modicum of self-disclosure. Most abuses are direct consequences of unrealistic assumptions created when relationships are established between insecure, hurting clients and their unemotional, apparently secure therapists.

In guided self-change, a significant safeguard against abuse is the infrequency of sessions. In the beginning they should occur no more often than weekly, and less often thereafter. Again, this is because the emphasis of self-change guidance is on what the client does *between* sessions, rather than on the professional relationship that takes place during them. Regardless of what goes on in any kind of session, an unhealthy intimacy or co-dependency between client and counselor is much less likely to develop with infrequent meetings.

A further safeguard against abuse is implemented with the next requirement of guided self-change.

3. **An agreement to tape-record all sessions for the exclusive possession and use of the client.** This is the most significant technical innovation of guided self-change counseling, and I regard it as indispensable to the process. Its many advantages are dis-

cussed in detail in the previous chapter, and you will need to point out those advantages to any therapist who is reluctant to give this innovation a try. In the face of continuing reluctance, you may suggest that your first session be recorded for both of you to review in private, or review in part during your next session. Then the two of you could discuss any foreseeable problem with this use of tape-recording. If the therapist is not willing to try any of this, then ask him why. A therapist who flatly refuses any experimentation with tape-recording for the client's use is not a good choice for a self-change guide.

If you sense that a therapist is actually fearful about recording the sessions—a feeling which he may express only in terms of professional reservations—then you can point out that the tapes serve to document what actually occurs in sessions, therefore protecting a guide from being falsely or unfairly accused of misconduct. Of course, the tapes also provide the client with protection from abuse, since the guide will know that his exact input is on record and in the client's possession. Such safeguards are not the purpose of the tape recordings, of course— their purpose is to enhance the client's self-observing capacities during the process of guided self-change. But these safeguards do answer many of the objections that may be raised about other issues of self-change guidance, particularly in regard to increased self-disclosure on the part of counselors.

4. **More brainstorming of new attitudes and actions for you to attempt between sessions.** Guided self-change is dramatically different from psy-

chotherapy in that it spends a minimum amount of time exploring the roots of your problems, and a greater amount of time brainstorming, rehearsing, and encouraging the implementation of specific experiments designed to change unhealthy attitudes and behaviors.

This does not mean that your past is to be ignored or its significance diminished. After all, most resistance to change has to do with early learning associated with intense feelings of hurt, fear, anger, and loneliness. Defensive attitudes that protect against the recurrence of such painful experiences have become habits of your personality. It is difficult to detach yourself from what has become your familiar sense of self. Unraveling the background of these patterns can definitely assist you in learning novel and more satisfying ways of being. If nothing else, it helps you to see that your view of yourself was constructed for good reasons, although it would now be helpful to revise it.

But such insight is only a tool for change, not the change itself. Insight helps you design and undertake experimentation with new attitudes and actions. Practicing them is the key to lasting change. A guide can encourage you to innovate and practice, but his greatest value lies in his capacity to help you brainstorm and rehearse the necessary experiments in changing yourself. To do this, he must give more of himself than in conventional therapy, for he must be both a role model and a creative fountain of ideas. And to help you come up with sensible experiments, he will probably have to use examples from his own life and his observation of other people, even if he chooses to disguise them.

Paradoxically, a self-change guide is less responsible for your well-being than a conventional therapist. The guide isn't there to take care of you, but
to spur you on toward taking greater and greater
responsibility for yourself. This is ostensibly the ultimate goal of most existing therapies, but the point
in time at which it's supposed to happen is always
somewhere in the indistinct future, after a long
period of analysis or medical treatment has "cured"
you of your diagnosed disorders.

But I believe that the cure for most psychological
suffering is the process of taking on and acting out
loving responsibility for oneself. The route to such
responsibility is a courageous, value-guided path of
action. Thus, a potential guide must be ready to
help you do something positive as soon as possible,
and apply all his caring, experience, and expertise
to providing you with the most creative encouragement he can muster.

5. **An agreement to regularly review your agenda
for self-change**, based on your continuing self-
assessment. Ideally, this review should occur at the
beginning of each session, and will of course include
any experience with change experiments attempted
since the last session. The guide's comments and
questions about anything she feels important and
relevant will be a part of this review, but it is not her
role to impose her direction on the course of your
work.

This review process is another dramatic departure
from psychotherapy, wherein the therapist is
usually making notes about your progress but not
sharing them with you. Also, he has most likely

plotted a course of treatment of which you are not fully aware—a course of treatment that is more likely to fit snugly with his preferred diagnostic model than to serve your real, untheoretical needs. Many therapists may be skeptical that a new client in emotional distress can actually direct her own course of change, but it is important to remember that growth need only occur by one experiment at a time—in accordance with solid, heartfelt values. In fact, a wise guide can help a client devise a realistic, step-by-step agenda, without taking over or supervising its execution.

Most importantly, a guide must resist any tendency to privately diagnose a client and maintain a secret opinion about her chances for improvement —the kind of opinion that therapists often withhold until they feel patients can "handle the truth." For conventionally trained therapists, this will mean throwing a lot of theories and academically conditioned behavior out the window. A more spiritual and less scientific approach to psychological counseling will naturally result in a more open mind about clients' abilities to handle honest feedback, as well their potential to change in unexpected but positive ways.

I know from experience that clients can change dramatically after courageous experiments, thereafter bringing me progress reports of surprising growth. This was the case with Max, the anxious architect I described in Chapter 3 who found a way to get back to work that no one could have prescribed or predicted. (As you will see in Chapter 9, Max eventually got back to work in such a big way that his entire firm was later challenged to change in order to keep up with him.) Thus, a guide must be willing to follow the client's agenda and his unpredictable progress wherever they may go, giving freely of his insights, suggestions, and honest reactions—instead of trying to fit the client into a theoretically brilliant course of treatment.

Shifting from Mid-Therapy To Guided Self-Change

If you are excited by the ideas in this book and are already involved in a long-term course of therapy, you may be wondering whether it's possible to enlist your current therapist as a self-change guide. In most cases, this should be easier than introducing the idea to a therapist you've only just met, because you have the advantage of an established relationship. You can introduce the topic during one of your regular sessions, or you might consider writing your therapist a note and asking for a special session to discuss the possibility of changing your respective roles.

After all, your initiative probably reflects the growth you have accomplished in therapy so far. Now you can make it clear that you want to accelerate your process by courageously experimenting with new, value-driven attitudes and actions, guided by mutual analysis of your current feelings about yourself and your relationships. After discussing this book or the ideas it contains with your therapist, you may devise a plan for a gradual shift from your current course of therapy to a full program of guided self-change.

A good way to begin would be with a discussion

of the values of respect, understanding, caring and fairness—a discussion that would be taped for both you and your therapist to review before your next session. Several taped discussions of self-change fundamentals might follow before you undertake the first brainstorming of attitude and action experiments. In this way you can allow time for your therapist to become educated about this new form of psychological counseling, as both of you devise the particular style that will suit your objectives best. You will also be developing a new self-observant capacity from the review of your session tapes, a capacity that will stand you in good stead when your self-change experiments begin.

Keep in mind that habitual behaviors don't die any easier for therapists than they do for anyone else. A therapist who is used to withholding himself and diagnosing his clients will not let go of those tendencies overnight. In terms of initiative, you may even be a role model for him at times! The best of therapists, like all good teachers, admit that they learn the most from those they help the most. (Some of my clients have been especially inspiring to me as models of self-compassion, and in demonstrating the value of experiencing enough simple, carefree fun in life.)

But it is important to remember that you are now paying for the services of an enthusiastic, creative, and encouraging coach of change, and you deserve your therapist's unstinting commitment to making a major alteration in his own perspective and methodology, at least in your case. If you feel that he is too resistant or reluctant to evolve and keep up with you after a trial period of three to six months, then you may want to seek out another qualified therapist who has a good reputation but is known to be flexible and adventurous in his approach. Those who are afraid to change and grow are unlikely to be the best resource to assist your self-change process.

The Shock of the New

Whether you are a therapist or the client of one, you may find the whole message of this chapter a little shocking. The very idea that a person who is suffering from significant psychological difficulties could walk into a therapist's office and specify the kind of help she needs may seem wildly improbable. After all, the popular image of someone in therapy is someone who can't manage her life on her own anymore, someone who needs a doctor to fix her or take care of her mind until she painstakingly learns to cope again.

However, the idea that someone in therapy is "sick"—an idea for which psychotherapy itself must take responsibility—is rapidly changing. The contemporary variety of counseling modes, along with the massive growth of support and recovery groups, is making the pursuit of psychological growth and change a more commonplace aspect of our society's life. Self-help books over the last three decades have disseminated psychological concepts and language to an ever-growing audience, with the result that we no longer regard psychotherapists and psychiatrists as the exclusive masters of a secret knowledge of the mind. And as discussed in Chapter 4, psychotherapy has come under increasing criticism in recent years, tarnishing its once exalted reputation.

I think this is all to the good, as long as we do not succumb to cynicism and decide that there is no use for a professional, psychological helping relationship whatsoever. I am recommending guided self-change as a complete and practical mode of counseling that draws its strength from several currents of contemporary psychology and our common life: a growing sense of spirituality, a trend toward democratization of counseling relationships, and a desperate need for the restoration of values in our societal awareness.

In the realm of counseling, all these ideas point toward a new image of the person in search of psychological help. He is not "sick" anymore; he is a courageous seeker of a spiritually centered, value-driven way of life. He realizes that he can use his suffering to motivate and point himself toward novel ideas and ways of being. He can become someone new, someone who is more expressive of his inner spiritual essence.

For everyone motivated to change, the first step is to realize that we are not the same as our suffering; or, to put it differently, to experience pain is not necessarily to be deserving of it. With that self-observant capacity activated, there is no reason we cannot seek out and specify the kind of help that will help us grow most quickly, freeing us of self-absorption and painful stagnation. At the same time, we can help our helpers free themselves of false, useless ideas and outmoded, peculiar behaviors that only get in the way of human communication and evolution.

As a psychiatrist who has largely healed himself of his training, I'm happy to present these perhaps shocking ideas to the general public, in a tested system that I hope is immediately useful to counselors and clients alike. The next chapter will make clear that I certainly do not suggest dispensing completely with the therapeutic techniques and interventions that have proven useful for a variety of psychological problems. But I believe that therapists must learn how to explain and present therapeutic tools to their clients for use *at the clients' informed discretion* —and not as medical prescriptions that patients should swallow without question. That's another shocking idea you can gently discuss with any therapist whom you're helping to change.

CHAPTER 7:

When Is Therapy Appropriate?

Psychoanalysis is the disease it purports to cure.
—Karl Kraus

Is guided self-change suitable for everyone seeking relief from mental or emotional distress? Aren't many people just too confused or depressed to attempt courageous experiments with their attitudes and behaviors? Shouldn't such people be taken care of in therapy for a while, before they try to take responsibility for their own positive course of growth?

To answer such questions clearly, it's necessary to define exactly what therapy is. Strictly speaking, a person is receiving therapy when he is the largely passive recipient of a physical procedure (or medications) intended to reverse or improve a physically demonstrable condition that's considered to be a disease or disorder. As the *American Heritage Dictionary* more concisely puts it, therapy is a *"treatment for illness or disability."*

In my view, one person who pays another to listen and talk is not receiving therapy—no matter how helpful the conversation may be. Such a "talking cure" may be inspiring and educational, or it may be demoralizing and miseducational. Classic psychoanalysis turns the talking cure into a highly artificial and stylized form of relationship that may *appear* to be a sophisticated medical treatment, simply because it occurs in a therapeutic context and it's impossible to figure out what else it's supposed to be. As journalist Janet Malcolm wrote in *Psychoanalysis: The Impossible Profession*:

> *Since Freud's establishment of the psychoanalytic situation as we now know it, psychoanalysts have been wrestling with . . . its radical unlikeness to any other human relationship, its purposeful renunciation of the niceties and decencies of ordinary human intercourse, its awesome abnormality, contradictoriness, and strain.*

But Malcolm points out that Freud himself pursued a less exotic talking cure:

> *He conducted therapy as no classical Freudian analyst would conduct it today—as if it were an ordinary human interaction, in which the analyst could shout at the patient, praise him, argue with him, accept flowers from him on his birthday, lend him money, and even gossip with him about other patients.*

It could safely be argued that most of the great therapists (including Jung, Rogers, Maslow, Erickson, and Perls) accomplished their "curing" of patients in a similar manner—by being persons of great insight and compassion who risked a greater authenticity than had previously been given to those they helped. But whether brilliant or ordinary, stylized or natural, conversation is not therapy. Taking an aspirin *is* therapy. Discussing your life with someone, regardless of their credentials or how much they charge you , should be regarded only as counseling—a process in which someone *influences* another, hopefully in a helpful way.

Why do I believe this distinction between counseling and therapy is worth making? It's critical because the concept of psychotherapy implies that its "patients" suffer from mental disease or emotional disorders which the therapist is responsible for easing or eliminating. Thus, the patient tends to have an expectation that he will be relieved of the difficulties in his life—those difficulties having been given medical labels such as "atypical depression" or "primary affective disorder"—and that he is responsible only for cooperating with the therapeutic treatment that will be applied to him.

Life would indeed be simpler for everyone if this model of psychological healing worked. But the "emperor's new clothes" of psychiatry and psychotherapy is that *no cure exists* for any existing diagnosis of mental and emotional suffering. Successful but limited therapies—from drugs to bodywork—which ease particular psychological symptoms do exist. But the closest thing to a cure for most forms of serious psychological suffering is a permanent change in the way one conducts one's life—and the changes in feelings and self-concept that occur as part of that process.

The same is true, surprisingly enough, in general medicine: Very few completely curative treatments exist. Some surgical and medical treatments help, sometimes immensely. But most treatments are not that effective, and many people are more injured than helped by side effects and complications. Nothing works better than long-term prevention and rehabilitation, both of which require the adoption of a healthy lifestyle. Again, a codependent collusion often exists between doctors with their treatments and patients who would rather be treated than take on the difficult job of maintaining a loving responsibility for themselves.

The aim of all psychotherapy and counseling is actually rehabilitation, i.e., a kind of learning that fosters or restores one's abilities to practice the art of successful living. So the most important question for a person seeking psychological help is, *"What kind of counseling will best accelerate my learning?"* Obviously, I believe that self-change-oriented counseling which is free of medical language and assumptions is far more effective than contemporary psychotherapy.

However, there are worthwhile psychotherapeutic techniques which can be used to great advantage by a client in consultation with a self-change guide. Later in this chapter I will address the usefulness of psychological and related therapies in conjunction with guided self-change. First, it is necessary to make clear what guided self-change does *not* provide—and to define the rare situations in which it is not appropriate.

What Guided Self-Change Doesn't Provide

If you decide to pursue guided self-change with a professional counselor, you should not expect:

- *A deep, ongoing analysis of your history;*

- *A detailed exploration of your unconscious—through dreams, slips of the tongue, and so on;*

- *Intellectual and impressive diagnostic labeling of you, your experiences and behaviors;*

- *An expert to take over responsibility for improving the quality of your life by applying a special approach or technique;*

- *Permission to talk about yourself and your problems for a long time without risking any changes in your attitudes and behaviors;*

- *The opportunity to have frequent visits with a supportive, understanding, well-educated person who fulfills a parental role for you—and who enforces your participation in counseling;*

- *Frequent rescues from emotional crises by an on-call professional;*

- *Direct treatment and intervention on behalf of your survival and well-being (because you are unable to maintain a self-observant capacity or muster the initiative for self-change).*

As the last point suggests, guided self-change is not suitable for intervention in a severe psychological crisis, when one is completely overwhelmed with extreme emotional distress due to anxiety, depression, hypomania, hallucinations, delusions, or any disabling irrationality due to brain dysfunction. While suffering from such conditions, one will have neither the objectivity nor the self-regard necessary to be in charge of self-change efforts, with or without a guide.

But few people remain in such crisis states for very long, and whenever one has regained enough balance to recover his self-observant capacity—which is, after all, a fundamental aspect of human consciousness, not a special talent—then one can resume or undertake some kind of self-change effort. In the long run, guided self-change is much more likely than traditional psychotherapy to free people from medical and therapeutic dependence.

Self-Change and Severe Suffering

But aren't there some chronically disabled people, such as schizophrenics, who cannot maintain a useful self-awareness long enough to make self-change efforts rewarding? Mustn't someone else be in charge of their lives permanently? To answer such questions thoughtfully first requires that we examine carefully our perceptions of mental and emotional disability.

Many prominent psychiatrists—especially Jung, Szasz, and R.D. Laing—have suggested that much of what we regard as schizophrenia or psychosis actually comprises various forms of socially unacceptable nonconformity. When such nonconformity involves violent impulses, society obviously has the duty to prevent their expression by restraining potentially violent individuals. In many cases, however, people have been institutionalized for behavior that simply makes others intensely uncomfortable. Such behavior is often the result of exotic attempts at self-protection. As Laing said in his classic work *The Politics of Experience*, "Schizophrenic behaviour is a special strategy that a person invents in order to live in an unlivable situation."

Yet it is well known that "miraculous" recoveries can occur when psychotic or schizophrenic individuals are allowed to experience *livable* environments, wherein they can participate in relationships that exemplify the basic values of respect, understanding, caring, and fairness. In *The Seduction of Madness*, Edward Podvoll described the courageous and compassionate approach that he and his colleagues used with severely psychotic schizophrenics living in home environments, an approach named the Windhorse Project:

> The process of recovery in general, and from psychosis in particular depends on creating an atmosphere of simplicity, warmth, and dignity. When the team therapists together perform the actions needed to establish that kind of environment and tone, recovery begins to happen; **islands of clarity** begin to gather and flourish, and one can take his ease and rouse the confidence to recover.

I know from my own experience that very distressed individuals can also respond to the *modeling of self-respect*. When I did one-on-one counseling in a VA hospital with schizophrenics in the late Sixties, it was not uncommon for a patient to break off our conversation in order to speak with one of his inner voices. My training had taught me to respond to such interruptions by quietly observing the patient's behavior and making notes, perhaps also making a probing but nonthreatening inquiry in reference to what the patient's inner voice was saying. But such a response had always felt completely unnatural to me.

Instead, I usually told the patient, "Excuse me for a moment, but I thought we were here to have a conversation together. I'm not trying to talk on the phone at the same time I talk to you, so I'd appreciate it if you tune out your voices and give me your complete attention." This always got the patient's attention. If he lapsed again, I would simply remind him that I required mutual respect as a condition of our continuing to talk.

Before long, I had developed a rapport with most of the patients that eluded the other psychiatrists. The patients pursued me and asked for private time whenever I would visit the ward, even though I was not their primary psychiatrist. The reason was not my insight or a brilliant analytic technique; it was simply that I elicited respectful behavior from the patients by exemplifying the value of self-respect. Thus, the patients recognized a strong ally who believed in their capacity to manage their demons.

As I've said before, I know that respect, understanding, caring and fairness are the fundamental values that anchor our self-awareness to our inner, self-directing, spiritual creativity. Show me any form of insanity not entirely caused by organic factors, and I will show you a human consciousness suffering from the absence or serious distortion of these values.

A self-change guide can help anyone begin the journey to restoring these values by exemplifying and explicitly discussing them . This alone will help many severely distressed people find and expand what Podvoll calls "islands of clarity"—and what I would call moments of compassionate self-observation that can occur in even the worse episodes of psychosis. A single island of clarity is an excellent place to begin the guided self-change process, whether a person is institutionalized or struggling to cope in the outside world.

In the near future, I sincerely hope that institutionalized mental patients are afforded access to self-change guides, or given an introduction to the process by progressive therapists who have learned and used its principles.* Self-change principles will also have enormous usefulness for counselors working with the substantial proportion of homeless people who are believed to be mentally "disturbed." As many homeless activists already know, one thing that disturbs the homeless is the feeling that they are shut out of a society whose values are topsy-turvy—the most obvious example being the worship of individual wealth over social well-being.

While political action can be an important part of regaining self-respect for many homeless individuals, activism alone can be too frustrating to provide sufficient encouragement for the long haul of rehabilitation and reunion with society. Troubled homeless individuals who receive counseling also need coaching in smaller, concrete steps toward reasserting values in their lives—those steps being personal, easily "winnable" experiments in behavior and attitude.

Because guided self-change does not require a special and expensive relationship developed between client and counselor over a long period of time, it could easily be applied to "one-shot" counseling contexts for the homeless—and for other

---

*The social learning programs increasingly available to chronically disabled psychiatric outpatients and their families are quite helpful, and entirely consistent with the guided self-change approach.

people whose access to regular psychological counseling is severely limited. This is just one realm in which the principles of guided self-change could be applied with great social rewards; others are discussed in Chapter 8, "Self-Change and the Human Future."

What is Incompatible with Guided Self-Change?

Guided self-change can be combined with almost any therapeutic technique, and people in almost any form of therapy can also be pursuing guided self-change, given the cooperation of their therapists. Curiously, the only forms of psychological influence that are incompatible with the guided self-change process are classical psychoanalysis and cult indoctrination. The reason is the same in both cases: Classical psychoanalysis and cultism each require a fundamental displacement of personal responsibility onto the analyst or cult leader. A very special relationship ensues in which the patient or follower is induced to accept either religious or scientific beliefs about her own nature (as well as the nature of reality at large), and her psychological growth is thereafter measured in terms of how completely she accepts those beliefs.

For instance, a woman in a cult may have a dream that her guru or fellow cultists tell her is evidence of her spiritual progress, or lack of it. The same woman in psychoanalysis may be told that her dream is a sign of her sexual insecurity. Either way, an important part of the woman's internal experience is interpreted in such a way as to support the belief structure of the cult or analysis.

In contrast, a good self-change guide would listen carefully to a client's dream, ask her how it might be related to her ongoing growth work, and whether it indicates progress or some changes she might make in her real-life experiments. If she wished to pursue deeper interpretations in pursuit of greater understanding of her unconscious life, her guide would direct her to the best available resources.

I do not mean to imply that either psychoanalysis or cults are necessarily entirely negative psychological experiences to be avoided at all costs. Various religious cults have received enormous negative publicity in this country, and the conclusion is often drawn by the press that controversial gurus and preachers are merely shameless hucksters devoid of any real wisdom. In fact, the story is usually more complicated than that.

It is possible for a spiritual teacher to pass on profound insights or directly induce significant altered-state experiences in his followers, and yet still be an emotionally immature and morally unscrupulous individual. Certain people can achieve important psychological growth under the sway of a cult, particularly at stages of adolescence or young adulthood—as long as the displacement of personal responsibility does not go on too long. It is also important to realize that such widely accepted institutions as traditional religions, the military, and corporate business use elements of cult indoctrination to both good and bad ends.

Likewise, the peculiar intensity of classical psychoanalysis can be beneficial to people who, born with exquisite sensitivity and exposed to severe emotional abuse as children, find themselves incapable of accepting their worth as adults and of allowing sustained intimacy. Nowadays, so-called "narcissistic" or "borderline psychotic" clients have become the predominant group seeking some form of psychoanalysis.

Other clients of psychoanalysis are often highly functioning people who are dissatisfied with their lives, despite considerable achievements and fortunate circumstances. For those who can afford an hour a day for up to five times weekly over two to eight years, psychoanalysis offers an engrossing exploration of one's dreams, memories and feelings in the company of an intelligent if somewhat remote guide. Despite significant discomfort, highly functioning people may be quite resistant to the idea of changing their attitudes and behaviors. Thus, the insight that can be afforded by long-term psychoanalysis may be a necessary precedent for self-change —or insight may be all they wish to achieve. I would advise people that they can achieve far more insight at far less cost through the self-change process. But few if any psychoanalysts would condone a client's attempt to follow both approaches simultaneously.

Guided Self-Change and Drug Therapies

During the last few years there has been a growing controversy over whether psychologists without medical degrees should be allowed to prescribe drug therapies. I think this controversy is going in exactly the wrong direction. The question is not whether to increase or restrict access to drugs, but how to dramatically reduce the need for them among people in therapy and counseling. In a nation plagued by a host of problems related to the use of illicit, mood-altering drugs, it would seem important that our psychologists and psychiatrists begin to focus their efforts on how to free people from dependence on prescribed mood-altering agents—because the lessons learned would surely be applicable to illegal drug use as well.

It is true that drugs can ease many dysfunctions and discomforts: hallucinations, delusions, manic or hypomanic episodes, severe depression, anxiety, even obsessions and compulsions. But although medications can shorten and soften the severity of such sufferings, it is important to remember that *no drug cures any psychological condition*—and all drugs have side effects, some of which are severe and irreversible.

While some psychiatrists pay lip service to the idea of minimizing drug therapy, many of them behave oppositely. This is due not only to the strong inducements they receive from the drug industry, but also to their patients' demands for immediate relief from suffering. The incentives to retain patients who are accustomed to drug usage and try out new, heavily marketed substances can overwhelm the moral incentive to encourage people to find a way of life that is drug-free. This goes on despite the fact that claims for the efficacy of new drugs are almost invariably overblown, and their side effects are generally understated.

Of course, the primary inducement to prescribing drugs is the medical model of therapy itself. As long as all forms of psychological suffering are seen as symptoms of disease—rather than warning signals of living out of balance—then the tendency to *treat* without *understanding* suffering will remain powerful. The result of long-term treatment of unheeded warning signals is drug dependency, with all of its attendant dangers and mind-altering effects.

As a recovering psychiatrist who now works chiefly as a self-change guide, I rarely prescribe drugs. Often I do work with people who are under treatment by other psychiatrists—people who are usually referred to me because conventional therapy is enabling them only to cope with their lives, rather than fostering any real fulfillment.

Andrew was in his late fifties when he came to me with a history of severe manic-depressive episodes which required constant and heavy medication, supervised by his wife and psychiatrist. He required hospitalization almost yearly, and had recently suffered a full-blown manic attack that required electroshock treatment in order to circumvent a rare, life-threatening manic fever. Andrew suffered other episodes of severe anxiety which expressed themselves in dangerous physiological symptoms. So it was not surprising that he led the life of an invalid —as did two of his children who also had significant psychological difficulties.

Andrew and his wife came to me in the hope that a self-change program might help him reduce his anxiety attacks and decrease his need for medications. It soon became clear that he had led a cloistered life long before he became dramatically troubled, partially because a large inheritance had removed him from the typical concerns of making a living. This tendency had been reinforced by the powerful social expectations of his family and peers, which had taught him to suppress his true feelings. As I got to know Andrew, I began sharing with him my hunch that his inner spirit was the opposite of his passive daily self. I suspected that he was born to be sensitive, independent, and highly opinionated. But to find out what his inner self was really like, he would have to undertake some experiments designed to give it a voice.

We agreed that the best thing for Andrew to try at first was keeping a daily journal in which he would write whenever he started to become "worried." To him, being worried meant experiencing very uncomfortable feelings that he took as evidence of his illness (officially diagnosed as Primary Affective Disorder). I asked him to consider the possibility that he had bad feelings whenever something in his life was not right for him, and that his inner spirit was speaking in an angry code to him through those feelings. Andrew was comfortable with the idea of his inner spirit, although he had never thought it might be trying to tell him things every day.

In learning to notice and write his feelings down, Andrew was literally stunned to realize that he became unhappy and anxious when asked to do things he didn't really want to do. All his life he had meekly assented to the demands of parents, wife, and friends, and his real reactions to unfair demands were always delayed, squelched, or swept under the rug—until they began erupting as the mysterious symptoms of his "mental illness." As he began to see the connections between his passivity and his problems, Andrew began to suspect, as I had, that his genuine spirit was proud and defiant. (To this day, he still becomes embarrassed when I point out that his private opinions and increasingly independent actions confirm that he's much stronger than he usually lets on.)

Gradually, Andrew was able to move from merely noting his feelings to acting more courageously to change his way of living. One of his most notable experiments was to go shopping in a supermarket by himself—the first time he had ever undertaken such a practical, caretaking task. This experiment was a partial success only because his wife became anxious about being left behind and joined him half-way through his expedition. Later, however, he was able to go out in the world on his own and gain further, very valuable experiences of independence and self-assertion.

The road to change was not smooth, of course. During one difficult phase of learning, Andrew had to survive a seven-month period of separation from his wife—who left because her husband's changes made her feel that she had previously been wasting her life by unnecessarily taking care of him. As such co-dependency issues were resolved, however, Andrew and his wife reunited.

Two years after our first meeting, Andrew is now on relatively small doses of medication that he adjusts himself, keeping in touch with the prescribing psychiatrist chiefly by phone. He is much more involved with the life of the world at large, and has even become involved in community volunteer work. Before guided self-change, Andrew's prognosis was not good; he looked like a candidate for repeated hospitalizations and heavy drug usage for the rest of his life. Because he was able to contact the wisdom, courage and originality of his real spiritual self, however, he has a very good chance of ultimately finding a drug-free way of life.

This is an example of how guided self-change can be pursued simultaneously with an existing program of drug therapy. I would be the last to suggest that people with a serious drug dependence should go "cold turkey" before attempting self-change experiments, and I cooperate with psychiatrists who are sophisticated in drug therapy and comfortable with my guided self-change philosophy whenever I think it can be useful to clients. No one should suffer needlessly, and I try to keep my clients informed of the full range of therapeutic techniques and interventions that might be helpful to them.

This may include extreme measures. I once helped a client arrange an electroshock treatment during a period when he could not guarantee to me or his family that he would not commit suicide before our next consultation. He much preferred outpatient electroshock to hospitalization, despite its memory-disabling side effects. This was the only time I have recommended electroconvulsive therapy in twenty-seven years of practice. A year later, this client, his family, and myself are all delighted that I did suggest it, for the curtailing of his suicidal phase proved to be the beginning of a rapid self-change process for this client.

Many progressive therapists have forsworn the use of electroconvulsive therapy (the city of Berkeley, California, actually outlawed its use within the

city limits), and I think it can be practically compared to hitting someone over the head with a ham-
mer. However, it has been conclusively shown that
this crude treatment can temporarily erase suicidal
tendencies and reverse certain life-threatening physiological expressions of distress, such as the type of
fever Andrew once experienced. Therefore, I would
not rule out electroconvulsive therapy as an option
for clients under very severe distress. But I would
make sure that they fully understand its considerable side effects, and that it is not undertaken
without their full and informed consent.

Guided Self-Change and Other Kinds of Help

Of course, most people seeking change in their
lives will not have need of extreme therapeutic
measures, and I believe that a broad acceptance of
guided self-change principles would dramatically
reduce the usage of mood-altering drugs among
people currently in psychotherapy. One reason is
that guided self-change can easily incorporate so
many other approaches to relieving suffering and ac-
celerating psychological growth.

My philosophy is to use or recommend anything
I've heard of that makes sense and is relevant to a
client's needs. I will also send clients on research as-
signments about novel or unusual approaches when
I don't have any information about them at hand.
This fits perfectly with the self-change emphasis on
clients' real-world experimentation. A self-change
guide should be a well-educated and well-connected

coordinator of resources, but not the only source of wisdom.

Traditionally, psychotherapy has operated as a *centripetal* methodology. This means that the energy and attention expended in therapy continually focuses on the therapy itself, particularly on the sessions between therapist and client. Very little of the rest of the world intrudes, except as a subject of therapeutic discussions. By contrast, guided self-change is centrifugal: Its energy is constantly moving outward and embracing more and more of the world.

That's the primary reason why guided self-change requires fewer consultations, and usually ends much sooner than conventional therapy. When the energy and intent is focused on how the client lives in the outside world rather than how and what he talks about in therapy, then before long the client will devise or re-establish a way of living in the world that needs no further coaching.

Along the way, other kinds of help that I may recommend to clients include:

- **Alcoholics Anonymous (AA) and other addiction recovery groups.** I've sent countless people to AA and similar groups, and I strongly recommend that they be persistent in finding the particular group that seems to serve them well. This can mean going to as many as ten meetings (possibly with ten different groups) rather than one, before deciding that such a group is not a useful resource. It's well known that people resist joining such groups when they are not yet ready to admit their addictions.

- **Peer and support groups** for sufferers of both psychological and physiological difficulties, from agoraphobia (fear of being out in public) and eating disorders, to Parkinson's or Alzheimer's disease. These groups provide valuable sharing of empathy and information available only from people going through the same kinds of experiences. A growing field for support groups is "inner child work," where people can learn to directly experience and work through childhood traumas, rather than leaving it up to a therapist to analyze them. (It's important, however, to make sure that an inner child group goes beyond the uncovering and expression of anger, to the healing of one's wounded inner spirit. To stay stuck in blame and a sense of early loss will only poison one's spirit further.)

- **Detox, wellness, and holistic health centers** for people who need to clear addictive substances and other toxins out of their body. I believe these centers are vastly preferable to hospitalization in most cases.

- **Hypnosis and self-hypnosis** for the control of anxiety and learning of certain behaviors. In most cases, I refer people to hypnotists for the sole purpose of learning self-hypnosis.

- **Behavior modification techniques** for people with isolated as well as more generalized phobias. Specialists in this field can help people learn how to deal with phobic stimuli through repeated exposure in a context of relaxation.

- **Outward Bound and similar challenge groups** for the learning of self-sufficiency and physical confidence. This alternative can be particularly helpful to people who have grown up over-protected —a condition which can be worsened by the conventional therapeutic environment. Classes or groups dedicated to various martial arts or performing arts may be helpful as well.

- **Yoga, massage, bodywork, and meditation** for release and control of anxiety, hypertension, and too much mental activity. I regularly refer clients to a yoga teacher I know, and many people have said it was one of the most useful referrals they ever received. A conventional psychiatrist might well rely on drugs, with or without psychotherapy, for the treatment of anxiety, hypertension, or mental obsessions. This would not only burden people with an expensive habit and the risk of serious side effects, but also deprive them of the opportunity to learn a time-tested discipline of health and self-development.

If You Picked Up This Book . . .

. . . then you're capable of taking on the challenges of guided self-change. The same is true for anyone who walks into a therapist's office under her own steam—even if she is under considerable duress, or seeking help at the insistence of a spouse, parent, or friend. It's fairly difficult for most people to ask for psychological help for the first time in their lives, and that request actually represents the beginning of a self-change process. Unfortunately, most conventional therapeutic environments actually slow down the process that people have courageously initiated, by encouraging them to become more passive and think about their problems for a very long time before they risk acting again.

By contrast, guided self-change provides an environment in which the relevant question is, *"What shall you do next to improve your life?"* The self-change consultant should always be asking, *"How can I help you help yourself?"* In that context, any therapeutic technique or technology that seems relevant, safe, and accessible is appropriate for use. But only rarely, I believe, will conventional courses of psychotherapy or psychoanalysis actually be preferable to guided self-change.

In the popular view, therapy is something you reluctantly undertake when everyday life has just gotten too tough, and you need professional help merely to be able to cope again. Hardly anyone expects therapy to propel you forward into a much happier, more challenging, and more altruistic way of life than you've ever known before. But guided self-change is a process that recognizes the human spirit's deep desire to be fully engaged in such a journey. Thus, it has the potential to lead you well beyond personal problem-solving—and help you learn to use the restless energy of your native spirit to change the world even as you're changing yourself.

PART III

HOW CHANGING YOURSELF
WILL CHANGE THE WORLD

Part III
PROLOGUE:

Welcome to a World of Change

The human race is on the eve of discovering a new world. It is not an unexplored continent nor a nearby planet; nor is it a super-technological realm of "future shock." Rather, we stand at the boundary of our own inner world. We are just beginning to look deeply into the real "human nature," and realize that it is not our invention. We may have disguised it with false ideas about ourselves, or shut out its quiet voice, but we have not altered or destroyed the spirit within us.

That spirit is linked to the mystery of all creation, and it is impossible for us to know the exact origins of something we did not create. It is not even important that we know, although we will always be curious. But we are just beginning to realize that we will be told everything we really need to know if we begin to pay attention to that still, small voice within.

This is the voice of human compassion, generosity, and joy. It is the voice that can help us make every daily, practical decision with deep, instinctive wisdom. This is a voice without fear, and a voice that needs no self-defense. When we genuinely speak our love, this is the voice that is coming through. And though it can seem at times to have no effects on a world of conflict, misunderstanding, and grief, this voice brings us the news of our greater reality.

To give up our troubled world and face reality, we must enter the world of change. This means relinquishing negative and limited ideas about who we are. It also means relinquishing all the narrow, conventional motivations—greed, self-protection, superiority—that support and prolong our false ideas. In their stead, we must accept fundamental values like respect, understanding, caring, and fairness, which serve to anchor our daily self-awareness to the timeless spirit within.

In the world of change, we will surrender the familiar in order to experience the magnificence of our potential. This will require great courage at first, because we will have to sort through the confusion of our feelings and try out strange new ways of thinking and behaving that are in accord with values of our inner nature—instead of being driven by our fears and doubts. As we all become more accustomed to the process and rewards of changing ourselves, the work will become easier because we will support each other in it. Our families, schools, businesses, and institutions will all be centers of self-change and learning.

Eventually, we will recognize that all the problems we may face are simply learning tasks, for we will understand that learning and teaching are the only purposes of life on earth. We are here to learn who we really are, and share our growing knowledge with each other. This learning is the route to genuine happiness and an abiding peace. In the world of change, we will make our spirit welcome, and our spirit will welcome us home.

CHAPTER 8:

Self-Change and the Human Future

The goal of the cold war was to get others to change their values and behavior, but winning the battle to save the planet depends on changing our own values and behavior.
—Lester Brown,
State of the World 1991

How does it actually feel to change? Here are the words of three of my self-change clients,* as they talk about their own experiences:

Andrew, the withdrawn and passive veteran of electroconvulsive therapy, who came to self-change counseling to reduce his need for psychiatrically prescribed drugs (see Chapter 7):

"I was in recovery from a severe attack of hypomania when I first came to see Tom. I thought I just wanted to learn to accept my illness, and to learn how to deal with my memory loss from electroshock. I didn't realize how low my self-esteem was, and I wouldn't have said that's what I wanted to work on. But I realize it now.

"I had been to three different psychiatrists before, but the experience just didn't compare. Psychiatrists

---

*As interviewed by D. Patrick Miller

basically don't say anything; you do all the talking. In our sessions, Tom suggested doing things differently, and talked about learning to act on my feelings. We role-played a lot of the things I needed to do, which gave me an idea of how to handle things on my own.

"When I listened to the tapes of our sessions, I could take notes on how to write a letter, how to bring up a subject with somebody, all of the things that were difficult for me. It was wonderful to have the tapes because there were so many things that I hadn't caught or absorbed in our times together. I got the fullest measure of our session time when I reviewed the tapes, and I always looked forward to listening to them.

"I remember once having a conversation with my son, and afterwards realizing that I was unhappy because I had not accurately stated something that I felt. So I went straight back to the phone and called him, and corrected what I had said earlier. That's an example of the new things I learned to do. I did a lot of them with my wife, which really changed our relationship in a positive way. Once you get started doing things in a new way, then it becomes a part of you. In the past, I just didn't know how I felt, so I couldn't do much about anything. I pretty much swallowed whatever I felt. So I had to learn to recognize my feelings so that I would be able to act.

"As things progressed, I did new things without a lot of hesitation because I knew I would have peace and be pleased with myself afterward. When I would go back and report to Tom what I had done, he really cheered me on. Reinforcement helps a lot.

"I got into a growth pattern with guided self-change. That I like very, very much. My new volunteer project is kind of scary; I'm unfamiliar with something like this. It's a big thing for me to make a two-year commitment, because I've never done anything like that before. But I have a different attitude about trying things out than I used to. I'm willing to try it, no matter what happens. If it doesn't work out, it doesn't work out—I can handle that."

Max, the architect who overcame a paralyzing anxiety about his job through courageous experiments in communication with his co-workers and clients (Chapters 3 and 8):

"For me, changing meant facing up to things. It was both frightening and exciting. There were some things I had been avoiding like crazy, and Tom pushed me to do some things that he told me would be incredibly uncomfortable. The fact that he warned me was actually helpful, because I didn't know why I was frightened.

"I tended to think there was something wrong with me if I was scared. After we talked things over I could tell myself, 'Maybe I'm not a total jerk if I'm frightened—here's a guy who says he's been through similar experiences, and he's an experienced counselor.' That gave me some comfort. Then I could say to myself, 'Alright, I'm afraid to do this, but there's a reason for being afraid that I've talked about. I'm not just a faulty human being.' All this was helpful at the stage of just looking at what I needed to do.

"I'm fifty years old, and I had been head of a department at the firm that's now headed by a thirty-three-year old. Part of my facing things was to go to him one day and admit that there was a project I simply hadn't done. It was a minor project, but a big block for me, something that I had just stared at for a long time. It took me a long time to get up the courage to go in there and say, 'Look, I screwed up. You're thirty-three years old, and I'm fifty, and at one point I was training you . . . but I have to confess that I really messed this thing up.'

"This was incredibly humiliating—not just to do it, but to come to work the next day knowing that everybody knew what had happened. But I was glad I did it; it was something I had to do. Along with other steps I'd taken earlier, this made me feel freer about work. Humiliating as it was, I could say afterward, 'Hey, I'm still alive. The building's still standing. I can do this again, and face whatever I have to face.'

"It does get easier to change with experience. I still worry sometimes, particularly that I'll slide back to the way I used to be, and the way I used to feel about myself. But I do feel a hell of a lot better. Now I'm working on getting closer to people in my friendships.

"One of the things I experienced at first was how odd it was to feel different. 'Have I put a new person in my body? Am I that changeable? Does this mean that I don't have a real personality, since I can change large parts of it?' That's an almost inhibiting feeling that happens at first, but I've felt it less and less over time. I'm certainly becoming more comfortable with the revised me. Sometimes I still have a problem with looking over my shoulder and thinking, 'Boy, if you start feeling too good about things, it's gonna blow up in your face.' But that's happening less and less, too.''

Ellen, the young woman who stopped both her drug abuse and shoplifting habit to return to school and begin her career (prologue to Part II):

"I had seen several psychiatrists before meeting Tom. Usually, psychiatrists just stared at me and didn't say much; if I brought out my feelings, they didn't know what to do about them. Tom really wants you to learn to handle your own feelings. Also, he lets you know what he feels about how you're treating yourself. Without that I might not have ever come out of the shell I was in.

"Tom once said something that really surprised me, something that I cried tears of happiness about when I understood: 'You can feel good about yourself all the time. Always feeling bad about yourself is not the right way to live.' I can count on one hand the number of times I felt really good before we started working together, and now it's a way of life. And it's become my nature to be honest. It's absurd to think of living any other way. I've learned how to take care of my spirit, instead of beating it up.

"It's becoming more natural to ask myself before I do anything, 'Will I feel proud of myself? Is this right or wrong? How will I feel about myself after I do this?' The whole idea that what you do directly affects how you feel about yourself—I just wasn't aware of that before, because of my family background.

"The biggest changing was very quick with me.

It was between one session and the next when the commitment not to steal really sunk in, and I could just do it. I can't explain that; something clicked inside me and I suddenly understood about looking ahead to see if I would be proud of things I did. Now I'm a totally different person than before. What I was doing before was absolutely nothing. Now I know that without my goals, I'm nothing and I can go nowhere. Before, I knew where I wanted to go and that I would have to change to get there, but I had no energy or enthusiasm to do anything about it. I was all talk and no action. Now I'm all talk *and* all action.

"Change has become a habit. Change scares people, and it's easier to stay the way they are. I don't know if they have the tools to go about changing, because it's hard if you don't have some guidance. I can keep going with it because now I feel good about myself. Once it gets started, it snowballs . . ."

Self-Confrontation and The Moment of Responsibility

Because guided self-change allows the counselor's self-disclosure and invites courageous experimentation on the part of the client, some people may conclude that it is merely a "confrontational" style of therapy, in which challenge and emotional intensity replace the psychotherapeutic conventions of the counselor's neutrality and emotional distance. Such therapeutic modes do exist, although they usually derive more from a particular therapist's personality than any formal school or approach. Some residential drug treatment programs for adolescents have used confrontational techniques in a cultish environment, with decidedly mixed results. Whenever confrontation is used as an all-purpose technique or serves to satisfy a counselor's personal needs, it can be very dangerous to the psychological well-being of vulnerable people who are in need of strong but compassionate support.

Some of my clients regard me as aggressive, particularly in comparison to therapists they have known who maintain a "professional" detachment. Other clients are surprised to hear that I have such a reputation, because I respond naturally to them in a consistently gentle manner. A self-change guide is "supposed" to be neither aggressive nor remote; the process requires him to be *authentic*. Thus, he need not suppress his real reactions and opinions because of any professional restraints. But he must present his point of view in a way that maximizes his chances of being heard and being truly helpful.

When a client is chronically resisting a change she desires, or suppressing her own true courage, it is important for a self-change guide to help her undertake the process of *self-confrontation*, and face what might be called the "moment of responsibility." This is the moment when a person realizes that her present and her future are in her own hands—no matter how much she may have suffered in the past, or how many external constraints upon her seem to exist at the present time. It is the moment when she realizes that she must go forward with whatever skills and resources she has—and that they will be enough, not necessarily to achieve everything she wants in the short term, but enough to begin changing one step at a time.

Whatever a guide can do to help a client along toward these realizations is appropriate, as long as it arises out of his authentic concern for the client's well-being, is in tune with his real feelings about the situation, and honors the values of respect, understanding, caring, and fairness. No matter how well-intended, therapeutic manipulations that are out of sync with a counselor's genuine, caring response to a client will tend to undermine the client's trust in the long run.

An authentic response to a client's resistance to change may be a soft statement of compassionate understanding; a self-disclosing reminiscence of the guide's own resistance to change in a similar situation; a gentle reminder about the client's aspirations; or a provocative challenge to lose no further time before taking charge of one's own destiny. There is no set prescription or technique to be applied; a guide must rely on his instinctual assessment of critical moments in the relationship.

Of course, a professional guide's authenticity in the counseling relationship is a different thing than the authenticity of a friend with whom a client might discuss her problems. A client has a right to expect a guide's response to be informed by a greater depth, understanding, and experience, as well as a developed proficiency in the "art of candor." And in all cases, a client deserves to benefit from the guide's own affirmation of the self-change process.

Too many therapists privately subscribe to the

popular notion that "people can't change," and therefore settle for helping their clients learn merely to cope with problems they will never learn to transcend. But a self-change guide must necessarily be something of a rebel against a psychological status quo that locks people into patterns of suffering. *The more people believe that change is possible, the more possible it becomes for everyone.* A self-change guide must be dedicated to championing the possibility of more rapid and positive human growth and evolution.

Further Applications of the Self-Change Philosophy

As pointed out in the next chapter, the fundamental values and philosophy of guided self-change are directly applicable to business practices, and I believe they will prove applicable in many other realms of human endeavor as well. In fact, any philosophy of psychological health that is not universally applicable is crucially flawed, because it will not enable people to make the connections between their well-being as individuals and their functioning in the realms of business, health care, artistic and athletic expression, education, political activism, and spiritual practice. Leaving business applications to be discussed in detail in Chapter 9, I'd like to comment briefly on these selected applications of the self-change philosophy:

• **Health care**—The mounting expense of medical care and insurance, as well as the increasing complexity of modern medicine, are making it clear that the future of health care for individuals lies chiefly in their own preventive behavior. That will mean significant changes in lifestyle for millions of Americans who eat unhealthily, exercise too little, and are addicted to stress. There was an interesting comment on this subject in the March/April 1991 issue of *Yoga Journal* presenting the work of Dr. Dean Ornish, a Harvard-trained heart specialist who developed a program combining yoga, meditation, group support, and a low-fat vegetarian diet that has proven successful in reversing arterial blockage in patients with severe heart disease (published in the book *Dr. Dean Ornish's Program for Reversing Heart Disease*). As *Yoga Journal* assistant editor Anne Cushman wrote:

> *Skeptical colleagues asked Ornish why he was trying something so 'radical' as asking his patients to change the way they lived. Why didn't he try some thing more conventional? they asked. Like filtering all his patients' blood through a dialysis-like machine every week to remove the cholesterol. Or surgically splicing their intestines so that cholesterol-laden food would bypass most of the intestinal tract. Or administering high doses of potentially toxic cholesterol-lowering drugs. . . .*

It may not be apparent to everyone that self-destructive habits of lifestyle tend to go hand in hand with negative psychological states. But changing the latter often requires some alteration of the former, because the mind and body are inextricably linked—and both are infused with the human spirit. As Cushman notes in the same article, preventive approaches such as Ornish's address the whole of the human being—whereas high-tech medical interventions can only forestall physiological catastrophes:

For Ornish . . . even more important than the physiological transformations were the emotional and spiritual ones. Patients found that as their blood vessels opened, so did their feelings; as more love poured out of their hearts, more blood could pour in. As participant Robert Royall testified, "My heart is really opening now. The facades are falling down. And I can reach out and take people into my heart in an easier way than I could a year ago."

For medical doctors and health care practitioners, the shift to a self-care and prevention philosophy that minimizes the use of high-tech interventions will mean a less punishing and more humane medical education; less time and expense wasted on patients who presently demand medical attention instead of taking care of themselves; less vulnerability to malpractice suits, and therefore lower insurance costs; and a healthier balance between their practices and their private lives, as they necessarily become models of self-care for those they serve.

In the long run (and I hope it is not very long), I think we will see a profound shift in our ideas about physical illness and cure, as we come to understand that the great majority of so-called "diseases" are actually the long-term effects of ignoring messages from body and spirit about crucial imbalances in the daily conduct of our lives. Great strides are being made in this approach through the study of "psychoneuroimmunology" and other immunological disciplines, many of which are still in their infancy.

As modern medicine becomes infused with the ideals of self-care, prevention, and the wholism of mind, body, and spirit, we will have less need for expensive and invasive medical interventions, including hospitalization. We will become less worried about our vulnerability to illness, and more engaged in the daily maintenance of our health and happiness.

• **Artistic and athletic expression.** Modern America has become a society of incredibly sedentary and passive adults. We are willing to have our creative energy absorbed by television, which tends to present the lowest common denominator of artistic and dramatic expression. We provide a minuscule amount of public support for the arts in comparison to other Western democracies, and we express a great fear about the purposes and effects of art through periodic movements toward censorship. But the solution to such controversies is not the establishment of firm societal standards for artistic expression.

Instead, we must realize that we are all artists in some way, for art is yet another voice of the irrepressible human spirit. If we all become more familiar with the way the spirit speaks through us in art, we will have less fear of artistic expression by individuals who write, sing, or express themselves visually in provocative ways.

As a self-change guide, I know that many people suffer greatly from the suppression of their own creativity. As clients of mine have moved toward self-acceptance and the pursuit of their greatest possible happiness, they have often rediscovered or initiated an artistic pursuit that gives them a special kind of joy. "Art therapy" is rapidly becoming less of a specialized adjunct to psychotherapy, and more of a popular and accessible means of direct expression for all kinds of people in pursuit of greater self-understanding.

As we come to understand that art is a lot of fun and something we all can create, we will have less romanticizing of "Artists" as people who are forced to live peculiar or even tragic lives for lack of understanding from society. As each of us begins to listen to the messages from our unique inner spirit, we will all find our artistic voices—and our society will become wiser and more beautiful as a result.

Likewise, we are all potential athletes to some degree, because we all have a natural physical energy that needs to be expressed and explored. Our fascination with professional sports shows evidence of this desire, but we are too willing to pay admission to sporting events or watch them on TV in lieu of developing our own athletic grace and strength. At the other extreme, a comparatively small number of us abuse ourselves with excessive exercise, creating a different kind of imbalance between mind, body, and spirit.

My experience as a self-change guide convinces me that people on the route to recovering their psychological wholeness will establish their own balance between mind, body, and spirit. That is why I regularly ask my clients what sort of physical exercise and recreation they are pursuing, and it is not uncommon for their self-change experiments to include new physical activities or diet-and-exercise programs they have chosen. The psychoanalytic tradition, by contrast, has created an excessively mental sort of "couch potato." In the future, any form of psychological counseling that does not encourage the maintenance or enhancement of physical vitality will be seen as primitive and unintelligent.

• **Education**. Up until the early part of this century, the ideal teacher was seen to be someone who "filled the vessel of a student's mind." What filled the student's mind was the hard information and cultural standards that composed the limited knowledge of her society.

The pace of change and the massive growth of information in twentieth-century society have rendered this picture of education obsolete. In the present and the future, the role of the teacher must be to enable the release of a student's inner potentials—her curiosity, her spiritual drive to learn, and her special talents. This role is directly comparable to that of a self-change guide, who helps people dissolve any notions of their psychological or spiritual defectiveness in order to tap their inner resources for positive change.

The effects of a self-change philosophy for education will be far-reaching and profound in schools from kindergarten to university levels. There will be less emphasis on grading and comparative achievements, and more on the natural development of individuals at their own pace. There will be less sequestering in classrooms and more engagement with the everyday world—an idea explored by the late education writer John Holt in his last book *Instead of Education*, in which he called for a new "apprenticeship" system for teenagers. Such a system would allow adolescents to balance their school experience with the acquisition of meaningful skills passed on by adult teachers in everyday contexts outside the schools.

Holt was also a prominent leader of the growing movement toward "home schooling," which at its best encourages a more natural involvement of parents in their children's education than is presently allowed by "PTA nights" at public schools. In some progressive communities, home schools and public schools are beginning to cooperate and evolve together toward forms of education that are dynamically integrated with the community instead of isolated from it.

Ultimately, a self-change and "lifelong learning" philosophy for education could lead us toward the establishment of "community universities," in which open access to all levels of learning would be afforded to everyone on a walk-in basis. Whether one was looking for scientific data, art classes, or psychological counseling, the community university would be the place to go—and it would be used as frequently as modern suburbanites now visit shopping malls. How much better for our teenagers it would be if they were naturally drawn to congregate in a place of open and non-compulsory education, where they were encouraged to develop and explore their unique, inner talents in a "learningful" environment founded on the values of respect, understanding, caring and fairness. Instead of forcing children to go to school and telling them what they must learn, we can guide, encourage, and supply the resources necessary to facilitate children's inborn learning instincts, while reminding them that their future is their responsibility. With such a shift in emphasis, we might come to find that we have far more potential "whiz kids" in our midst than we have yet imagined.

• **Political activism**. The chronically low voter turn-out of our democracy reveals the extent to which many people have become disengaged from crucial political processes. Not surprisingly, the quality of our leadership has visibly suffered, and thus we tend to distrust the ethical standards of our politicians. Just like an individual addicted to psychotherapy, we end up turning our attention away from the larger questions of our societal well-being, increasingly focusing on strictly personal problems and goals. This means that the political process becomes more and more like a marketplace where well-heeled special interest groups and individual power brokers hold sway.

Application of a self-change philosophy would introduce a number of healthy changes to the political realm. We would begin by questioning and selecting our elected representatives on the basis of their dedication to long-term, fundamental values, rather than short-term, politically expedient "causes." To gauge our politicians' genuine dedication to values—which cannot be determined on the basis of ghostwritten campaign speeches—we would require more self-disclosure from our candidates, particularly in regard to their feelings about value-related issues and their personal history of self-development and change. In a change-oriented society, the *self-knowledge* of our leaders will be a significant issue in their selection and success.

On the citizens' side of political activism, it is clear

that we must learn to summon great courage to negotiate the critical issues facing us. Foremost among these are the pressing environmental crises that will inevitably require significant lifestyle changes in a society used to wasteful consumption of natural resources. Likewise, we must eventually come to face the facts about our continuing economic and racial inequities, and arrive at the same kind of "moments of responsibility" that come to individuals during the process of self-change. The comic strip character Pogo summed up the essence of social responsibility when he said, "We have met the enemy and he is us." It does no good to make war on this enemy—but he can and must transform himself.

• **Spiritual practice.** The flowering of "new religions" and Eastern spiritual techniques such as meditation during the last thirty years has had a substantial effect on Western ideas about religious practice and spiritual self-development. There is a growing acceptance of the "inner spirit" as a reliable guide for human growth and self-conduct, as opposed to the traditional, unquestioning acceptance of religious authority.

Contact with the inner spirit is a fundamental goal of guided self-change, of course, and it is also encouraged in the various forms of transpersonal, or spiritually-oriented psychotherapy. Although generally underreported and misunderstood by the press, America's new and increasingly personal spirituality is a major force encouraging our return to deeply felt values as a guidance system for individuals and society as a whole.

The contemporary spiritual teaching called *A Course in Miracles* suggests that "a universal theology is impossible, but a universal experience is not only possible but necessary." This means that people worldwide are never likely to agree about the nature of God and our cosmological origins, but we can all experience the truth of our inner spiritual nature. Discovering that truth has been called "redemption" or "being born again" in Western religions, and "enlightenment" or "self-realization" in Eastern traditions. Regardless of what one chooses to call it, the path to spiritual self-knowledge begins with the process of value-guided self-change.

As we approach the next century, the joining of psychological and spiritual paths to self-discovery will provide great rewards in human creativity and inspiration. The key to resolving or transforming the tremendous problems of our troubled species lies in the realization that we really can contact a source of magnificent wisdom and guidance within ourselves —a source whose origin we do not need to locate, but whose reality we desperately need to accept.

Considering the Possibilities

If there is any phrase that sums up my approach as a self-change guide, it is *"consider the possibilities."* I am always urging clients to consider the possibility that they can learn to look beyond their habitual pain and confusion, and fashion new lives for themselves that honor and exemplify the fundamental values of respect, understanding, caring, and fairness. I ask them to consider the possibility that they can learn to understand all their feelings as messages from their unique inner spirit—and that their spirit can lead them into more intimate and caring relationships, more rewarding work and play, and a greater sense of peaceful self-acceptance than they have yet imagined possible.

"Considering the possibilities" calls forth the two inner resources most crucial to human growth: *imagination* and *courage*. We must first be able to imagine our possible futures, and select the changes in attitude and behavior that will get us there. Then we must be ready to summon the courage for undertaking the step-by-step experimentation that change requires. We cannot consider our possibilities if we remain fixated on the past, or if we convince ourselves that we are fundamentally flawed, defective, or ill. And we will never experiment with new ways of being as long as we wait for change to happen to us, or for the rest of the world to change to suit us.

It is all too easy to look around us at the suffering and stupidity of humanity, and conclude that we are a doomed species. We have not learned to live without war, we have not learned to live in ecological harmony with the natural world upon which we depend, and we have not learned to share our resources and knowledge equitably among ourselves. But when these undeniable facts tempt us to conclude that the human condition is hopeless, we are not considering a crucial possibility: *We can change*. It's hard, but we can do it. This book is my way of wishing you Godspeed in your own self-change process, and helping you find the caring, dedicated, and dynamic guidance you deserve.

Please note: *This supplementary chapter will be of special interest to readers involved in business or personnel management, and to anyone curious about detailed applications of the self-change philosophy to the "real world" outside a counseling context. However, this chapter is not essential to an understanding of the guided self-change philosophy.*

CHAPTER 9:

Changing Business in Changing Times: The Ethical Route to Long-Term Profits

Respect Heaven and Love People.
—motto of the Kyocera Corp.

It may seem strange to find a chapter about business in a book devoted to changing the nature of the psychological helping relationship. After all, the basic theories and practice of individual psychotherapy have never been particularly relevant to the conduct of organizations and business.*

That fact speaks volumes about the shortsightedness of both therapy and modern business. By endlessly analyzing people's problems in a special environment closed off from the real world, psychotherapy encourages people to think excessively about themselves and their difficulties, when they really need to be learning how to make better decisions and communicate more effectively in the world at large. And when any business fails to take

---

*Even the group approaches such as T Groups and Gestalt, which have been tried, have never been incorporated into the mainstream of organizational values and practices.

an interest in the psychological health and growth of the people within it, it is condemning itself to mediocre performance or even failure in its market, due to poor morale, unreliable performance of its personnel, and competitive disadvantage in the labor market.

So there ought to be a common-sense connection between personal problem-solving, communication, and growth, and decision-making, teamwork, and continuous improvement in organizations. Due to their reluctance to espouse a set of guiding values and their emphasis on a pathological orientation, none of the current psychotherapies will ever provide that connection. Conversely, by its focus on personal experimentation with new attitudes, and its espousal of respect, understanding, caring, and fairness as guiding values in all aspects of work and personal life, guided self-change does make a clear connection between self-management and managing others.

That's why I've been able to expand my work in recent years beyond one-on-one counseling into the realms of organizational conduct and change. Presenting workshops on ethical persuasion, ethical decision-making, and strategic self-management for a variety of corporations and professional organizations,* I've been able to teach principles of change and success to individuals working together on common goals. At a time when the American economy is suffering considerable damage resulting from

---

*Including Foodmaker/Jack in the Box Restaurants, Blue Cross of California, San Diego Gas & Electric, Zions First National Bank, and the California Center for Judicial Education & Research, among others.

years of unethical policy-making and practices, the adoption of healthy, timeless values by both corporate and small businesses could not be more important.

In this chapter, I can hit only a few high spots of what I've learned, and begin to pass this information on to others. But everything I teach to organizations proceeds from two basic premises:

For any organization to thrive, individuals within that organization must be good at personal change;

and

The values of respect, understanding, caring, and fairness form the ethical foundation for quality in any organization.

If these premises surprise you or seem somewhat removed from the daily concerns of business as usual, please bear with me as I explain their practical applications. I hope it becomes clear that the principles of personal change and value-driven behavior are just as important to the long-term success of organizations as they are to the health and happiness of individual human beings.

Beyond the Profit Motive: The Learning Motive

In Chapter 3, I proposed the idea that learning is the spiritual purpose of our lives as individuals. As we approach the next century, the changing nature of our society will make it necessary for businesses and organizations to adopt learning as their primary motivation, too. As Peter Senge of MIT's Sloan School of Management wrote in his book *The Fifth Discipline: The Art and Practice of the Learning Organization:*

> *As the world becomes more interconnected and business becomes more complex and dynamic, work must become more "learningful." It is no longer sufficient to have one person learning for the organization, a Ford or a Sloan or a Watson. It's just not possible any longer to "figure it out" from the top, and have everyone else following the orders of the "grand strategist." The organizations that will truly excel in the future will be the organizations that discover how to tap people's commitment and capacity to learn at all levels in an organization.*

To inspire learning at all levels in an organization, there must be encouragement of change on the part of all individuals within it. This means that an organization must adopt a vision that goes not only beyond the profit motive, but also beyond the usual notions of providing a needed service or reliable product to the community. Rather than regarding employees as cogs in a machine who need only to learn their limited tasks and thereafter perform them obediently and efficiently, a business must see its employees as its most precious resources—whole human beings with largely unknown and untapped potentials to think, to learn, and to teach one another. The more those potentials can be drawn out and tapped, the better a business will be at changing with the rapidly evolving needs of its clientele and society at large.

In many ways, switching priorities from maximizing profit to maximizing learning is the exchange of short-term gain for long-term investment. The importance of thinking and planning for the long term is becoming plain in many areas of social concern, including ecological well-being, education, international relations, and the economy. In the Nineties, we all face having to pay the bills for a number of economic disasters—the collapse of the S&L industry and the junk bond market being the most recent major ones—caused by the irresponsible short-term, maximum profit-oriented thinking of the Eighties. Our economic crisis, regardless of how intense or long-lasting it proves to be, presents us with an excellent opportunity to review and analyze our past motives and methods, and thereafter attempt new, value-driven attitudes and behaviors in business situations.

Why Quality Decisions Pay

No one should fear, however, that adopting a primary learning motive for business and organizations means giving up the profit motive. In fact, it enables the possibility of making a healthy profit over a much longer time, since a learning business will keep pace with change in the marketplace.

The well-known ''boom and bust'' syndrome of Western business, in which new and successful companies tend to plummet and fail after rapid growth periods, is symptomatic of numerous ills, among them greed, a lack of vision by our business leaders over the past 45 years, and failure to keep learning and changing over the long term. Focused on achieving the maximum profits that are feasible at the moment, companies are caught up short when market forces shift abruptly. As Peter Senge notes, one third of the firms on the 1970 "Fortune 500" list had vanished by 1983. If unable to plan wisely for future contingencies, even the most successful companies will see their short-term profits sacrificed to change.

To anticipate change, we must be good at changing, both as individuals and as groups of individuals working in concert. A changing individual is guided by his inner spirit. To change and grow, an organization likewise must be guided by an explicit statement of vision that summarizes the group's highest purpose, and that inspires every member's spiritual development by being in harmony with his own personal values. To keep a group's vision from becoming an empty motto that has no practical applications, the group must anchor its daily operations to the same universal values that provide an individual with direction: respect, understanding, caring, and fairness.

This means that "doing the right thing" becomes the new way of doing business, so that all practical decisions become "quality decisions," and people treat each other in value-driven ways. Quality products and services flow automatically from organizations whose people treat each other in quality ways. In the long run, quality decisions and respectful ways of communicating do pay off, even as they may tend to moderate short-term profits for the sake of an organization's long-term health and optimal treatment of its members. The following flow chart outlines the relationship between quality decision-making, ethical influence, and the bottom line.

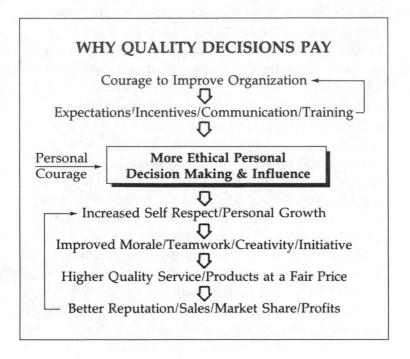

WHY QUALITY DECISIONS PAY

Courage to Improve Organization

Expectations/Incentives/Communication/Training

Personal Courage → **More Ethical Personal Decision Making & Influence**

Increased Self Respect/Personal Growth

Improved Morale/Teamwork/Creativity/Initiative

Higher Quality Service/Products at a Fair Price

Better Reputation/Sales/Market Share/Profits

The decision by senior management to make positive changes in an organization may be driven by fear of imminent failure, evidence of internal disorder (poor teamwork, unethical conduct, exodus of key personnel), or the desire to achieve better market positioning for the future. Regardless of the motive, instituting organizational change requires a kind of *courage* similar to that of an individual seeking help for psychological distress. By courage I mean doing what is right despite the risks and the fear that risk engenders.

Generally speaking, this courage must be implemented by an organization's high-level leaders and decision-makers, although the impetus for change may arise from lower levels. All too often, however, leadership's courage extends only to the declaration of new policies, quotas, or procedures (often still based on old familiar premises) that are unilaterally imposed on lower levels of the organization. In these ranks, people addicted to long-standing ways of operating tend to be suspicious of upper management's real and unstated intentions. The predictable results of this kind of "false change" include resistance, perfunctory obedience, confusion, increasing disrespect of leadership, and inconsistent application of executive decisions.

By contrast, quality decision-making requires that leaders endorse and inspire the courage to change at all levels of an organization. This is done through the leaders' *expectations*, real *incentives*, continuous two-way *communication*, and *training* in the skills required for quality management of self and others. The leaders' expectations of a company-wide quality orientation must be bolstered by a rigorous policy stating that everyone in the organization, from top to bottom, is to be treated with dignity at all times. Change and innovation can be reinforced by real incentives, which may include financial and other rewards for innovative suggestions and constructive criticism coming from employees. It's also important to grant employees latitude to experiment and fail without penalty.

Such a situation is a far cry from the present oper-
ation of many large corporations, where innovation
and constructive criticism from the bottom up are
more likely to be met with suspicion and outright
resistance—particularly from managers accustomed
to relying on their positional authority rather than
personal influence. But why encourage people to become embarrassing whistle-blowers or go elsewhere
in order to use their creativity?

To prevent chaos in a changing organization,
communication among all its levels, and in all direc-
tions, is of paramount importance. This places a special responsibility on a group's leaders, because it is
up to them to keep in touch with all levels of the organization and continually invite input and response. A corollary of good communication, by the
way, is that leaders must be proud of their abilities,
actually *enjoy* their work, and also enjoy listening to
and understanding what people think and feel, from
the bottom to the top of the organization. Continuous, positive change will be difficult and piecemeal
in any group effort where the managers are remote,
authoritarian figureheads who assert their authority
by pressuring subordinates to meet arbitrary quotas,
and by discouraging honest feedback, instead of
fostering morale by skillful listening and coaching.

Finally, organizations must train their people for
the process of change. This means coaching in the
fundamental skills of managing self and others—
decision-making and exerting influence in ethical,
value-driven ways. The eventual result will be the
growth of *more ethical personal decision-making and influence* on the part of all participants on a team—a
development that not only makes the team more

open to positive change, but also enables it to respond quickly and effectively to major crises.

A good example of a large corporation's ethical response to a crisis is the story of Johnson & Johnson in the Tylenol scare of 1982. When seven people died from taking poisoned Tylenol capsules, Johnson & Johnson managers all over the country had to react quickly and decisively. As Manuel G. Velasquez reported in his essay in the anthology *Essentials of Business Ethics*:

> *To a remarkable extent [the managers'] decisions were uniformly and instinctively aimed at protecting the public: local managers independently pulled lots of Tylenol capsules off local shelves, marketing managers halted all advertising for Tylenol, all managers joined in support of a full public disclosure of the situation, and a massive recall of all Tylenol capsules was launched (a move that cost the company an estimated $50 million after taxes).*

Velasquez attributes the uniform crisis response of Johnson & Johnson managers to the corporation's "systematic attention to inculcating in all managers the values embedded in the company Credo." The Credo, a statement of the company's vision, declares "our first responsibility is to the doctors, nurses, hospitals, mothers, and all others who use our products." Velasquez continues:

> *For several years the company had invested considerable time and resources into developing the Credo, communicating it to all employees and ensuring that it was genuinely integrated into every aspect of management thinking, including product choice, advertising, employee compensation, research, delivery times, costs, and financial reserves . . .*
>
> *Today, as a result of the trust and confidence that Johnson & Johnson's response created, the company has completely re-*

covered its losses. Sales of Tylenol are once again at high levels, and the firm is prospering.

The remaining four stages of the flow chart show clearly how ethical decision-making and influence can provide an organization with dynamic resiliency and the ability to consistently manifest a guiding vision. The *increased self-respect* and *personal growth* of group members who have been treated ethically and allowed to make ethical decisions leads directly to *improved morale, teamwork, creativity,* and *initiative.* These are invaluable qualities that simply cannot be "bought" or enforced by heavy-handed authoritarianism; rather, they are natural signs of what is usually called "team spirit," and might be more broadly called "organizational spirituality."

Such qualities within an organization naturally result in *higher quality service* and *products at a fair price,* which represent the extension of a company's fundamental values to its customers and society at large. Finally, the ethical process leads to a *better reputation, sales, market share* and *profits* over the long term—which feed back directly to individuals in a group in terms of self-respect and personal growth. The entire process is continuous and self-reinforcing, as long as an organization maintains a courageous willingness to embrace change and adhere to an ethical vision.

Continuous Improvement: The Cycle of Change

The next flow chart provides a way for both individuals and organizations to anticipate the inevitable stages of change in an ethical growth process.

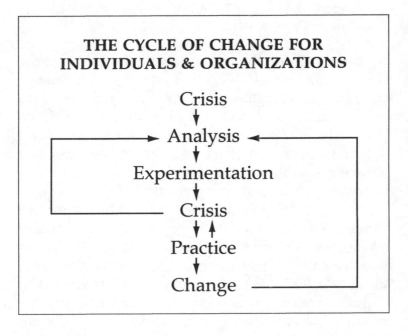

THE CYCLE OF CHANGE FOR
INDIVIDUALS & ORGANIZATIONS

Crisis
↓
Analysis
↓
Experimentation
↓
Crisis
↓ ↑
Practice
↓
Change

Almost all deliberate change is necessitated by some form of *crisis*. An individual makes an appointment with a counselor because some aspect of life has become distressing and unmanageable; a company considers a change in style or methodology because of a change in leadership, internal problems, or because its market share and profits are decreasing. What must follow next is a period of *analysis*, in which the immediate and long-term history of the organization and market conditions leading up to the crisis situation are carefully reviewed. In psychotherapy, this stage usually goes on far too long, or is actually never succeeded by the next stage of *experimentation*.

But in deliberate change by individuals, groups, or entire organizations, the task of analysis should be undertaken with the idea that experiments in new behaviors (or organizational methods) and attitudes (or policies) will follow. The nature and direction of these experiments will be determined not only by the analysis of past problems, but also by the application of values (or vision) and courage, in order to keep moving toward certain desired goals. This is where the process of quality decision-making applies to the process of positive change.

Real experimentation—as opposed to the re-labeling of former or traditional methodologies—inevitably leads to a new kind of *crisis*, or what Chapter 3 described in detail as the "awkwardness of change." The fear and discomfort of acting in novel, value-driven patterns will occur in organizations just as it does for individuals because the Familiarity Principle applies in both cases:

You cannot act or be treated in ways that are different from those you are used to—even if those ways are better—without becoming increasingly uncomfortable.

What eventually decreases the discomfort of change is repeated *practice* of new behaviors, methods, attitudes, and policies that survive the experimental process and prove their worth. Each repetition of a real-world experiment will vary slightly, sometimes inducing new "mini" crises that may call for analysis and inspire revision of existing experiments. In the midst of this process, real *change* will be happening—and it often takes place before an individual or group is fully aware of its presence or significance. But as positive change is recognized, it is important to subject it to further analysis—the kind of analysis that can rightfully begin with celebration and reward.

A Catalyst for Organizational Change: The Self-Changing Innovator

Anyone who has begun learning to change herself will have first-hand experience in innovation—and that experience is an invaluable asset for any learning organization. In his book *Intrapraneuring: Why You Don't Have to Leave the Corporation to Become an Entrepreneur*, Gifford Pinchot III defines a person who creates change and new ideas within an organization as an "intrapraneur":

> . . . any of the "dreamers who do." Those who take hands-on responsibility for creating innovation of any kind within an organization. The intrapraneur may be the creator or inventor but is always the dreamer who figures out how to turn an idea into a profitable reality.

In my counseling practice, I've observed that individuals who have begun to succeed in their self-change processes soon establish a momentum that is unstoppable. Not only do they have less and less need of my suggestions, but their fully-engaged creative spirit induces a pace of personal innovation that surpasses what I may have thought possible for them. Pinchot finds similar characteristics in those people who lead the way in organizational "intraprises":

> Intrapraneurs cannot be appointed and told to bring their zeal to bear on specific intraprises. Instead, managers should watch

for subordinates who express passionate beliefs in specific projects; then these subordinates can be empowered to act on these beliefs. . . . The system that recognizes and fosters intrapraneurship may only be legitimizing what is already happening. Managers need to recognize another potential benefit of encouraging intrapraneurship: the intrapraneur's commitment to an intraprise in which he or she deeply believes can shave weeks or months from the time required to execute that intraprise. When an intrapraneur gets going, the speed of work can be astonishing.

A self-changing innovator may also challenge an entire organization to undertake the kind of change process at which he has be come proficient on his own. I saw this happen with Max, the architect whose story was introduced in Chapter 3. Unable to face working when his self-change process began, Max eventually began contributing to his firm again through outside consultations with clients, before risking much time with colleagues at the office. But within two months, Max was able to return to work full-time, and his enthusiasm and efficiency were remarkable. So remarkable, in fact, that a crisis in cooperation arose among the firm's partners.

George was Max's working partner, who had picked up a lot of the slack for Max during his nonproductive phase. Now that Max had returned and was doing a greater share of work than he ever had before, George felt both unappreciated and outdone. He began to nitpick about Max's work, complaining to the senior partners, who decided that Max was becoming a new kind of problem—a high-risk overachiever. They called me, and asked for a consultation without the presence of Max, in order to decide "how to handle him."

But I declined to participate unless Max was invited to attend. I suggested to the senior partners that Max's new attitude and productivity could be viewed not as a problem, but as a "change crisis" reflecting the firm's problematic communication style. This new crisis presented all the partners with the opportunity to improve communication among themselves, so they might prevent serious partnership problems in the future. I further suggested that the firm could even learn something about how to improve its overall productivity from someone who was well on his way to realizing his maximum potential. Acknowledging the fairness of my suggestion, the firm's partners eventually decided to meet for a weekend consultation together, without any outside advisors.

This was a new experiment for an organization that had previously operated with a minimum of reflection and open discussion of long-term goals. At this writing, it's too early to tell where the experiment will lead—but I am confident that they will find a way to integrate and learn from the dynamic "intrapraneurship" of Max.

The Expansion of Business Values

As ethics, the learning motive, and long-term viability become widely accepted as organizational priorities during this decade, we are likely to see the vision and values of many businesses expand dramatically. This trend is already evident in such highly successful companies as The Body Shop, a British retailer of natural cosmetics and body lotions, and Esprit, the California sportswear firm—both of whom espouse strong ecological concerns, and have integrated these concerns into their marketing profile. Both firms also encourage their employees to do volunteer work for their communities while on the payroll. The Vermont ice cream makers known as "Ben and Jerry" have established a number of progressive employment policies, including profit-sharing and democratic decision-making methods, while diverting a percentage of corporate profits to various social causes—all the while increasing their market share.

By no means are these companies merely flukes on the lunatic fringe. One only has to keep an eye on major business advertising to notice that an increasing number of major corporations are capitalizing on their integration of an ethical emphasis in order to appeal to consumer concerns ranging from fair pricing and product reliability to environmental impact. While Nobel Prize-winning economist Milton Friedman has stated that "the social responsibility of business is to increase its pro-fits," such a narrow perspective will prove increasingly archaic in an information-age society in which values, ethical behavior, and a growing capacity to learn and change are in greater demand than investment capital.

With the disintegration of the Iron Curtain, the West has a tremendous opportunity to teach not only capitalism, but also a true and humane democracy to the societies of Eastern Europe. By throwing off their oppressive forms of government, they have proved themselves capable of instigating a magnificent experiment in change. As they look to us for guidance in entrepreneurship and self-government, we must be sure to teach and model something more lasting than short-term profiteering, unethical forms of influence, and thoughtless exploitation of human and natural resources. A world in the midst of many crises of change has more need than ever of the fundamental values of respect, understanding, caring, and fairness.

APPENDIX

Worksheets and Agreements for Guided Self-Change

The following four documents are used by Dr. Tom Rusk to help initiate the guided self-change process with his clients. They are included in this book as models for counselors who may be interested in adapting some or all of the aspects of guided self-change as described in this book.

I. *Life Performance Inventory*. This self-assessment questionnaire helps the client and self-change guide measure factors of stress in the client's life, including susceptibility, current symptoms and effects, and the client's proficiency in self-care. It also serves as an educational tool that helps the client become aware of all the factors involved in one's sense of well-being.

II. *Client Worksheet*. This document enables the client to identify and state his or her problems, needs, and goals at the inception of guided self-change. The course of the guided self-change counseling relationship is directed by the client's evolving needs and goals, instead of the diagnosis that would be made in conventional psychotherapy.

III. *Consultation Agreement*, Parts 1 and 2. These

contracts clearly establish the respective responsibilities of the self-change guide and client, thereby discouraging the therapeutic co-dependence that often arises in conventional counseling.

IV. *Tape-Recording Agreement.* This statement confirms that the client has agreed to the tape-recording of sessions, and is aware of the risks and cautions that should be kept in mind concerning the client's possession and review of the tapes.

These documents may be copied or modified without permission. If you are interested in updates, or further information on guided self-change, write or call Dr. Rusk at 4344 40th Street, San Diego, CA 92105, (619) 280-0335.

LIFE PERFORMANCE INVENTORY

Name _____

Therapist _____

Date _____

As your consultant, I'm asking you to fill out this questionnaire. It may be a tedious job, but it will give us both a baseline from which to consider possible changes. The ultimate goal is to find ways for you to improve your well-being and satisfaction.

The use of a questionnaire format for this kind of data allows us to make the best use of the valuable time we will spend on a person-to-person basis. Your identity on this inventory will be kept strictly confidential. Please mark an X beside the answer or fill in the blank where indicated. Thank you for your cooperation.

1. I am seeking counseling for help with
   0   family or couple problems.
   1   school problems.
   2   job problems.
   3   drug problems.
   4   alcoholism.
   5   sexual problems.
   6   mixed-up thinking.
   7   legal problems.
   8   other _____
       _____

2. I am
   0   single.
   1   married.
   2   remarried (state number of marriages _____).
   3   divorced.
   4   separated.

3. I have been in my current marriage for _____ years.

4. I have had _____ children.

5. The number of people living in my home, including myself, totals
   1   1 person.
   2   2 persons.
   3   3 persons.
   4   4 persons.
   5   5 persons.
   6   6 persons.
   7   7 persons.
   8   8 persons or more.
      Of these, _____ are children.

6. The language spoken most often in my home is
   0   English.
   1   Spanish.
   2   Italian.
   3   Portuguese.
   4   Other _____

7. Have you ever received counseling, therapy or psychiatric care?
   0   No previous care received.
   1   Yes, as an inpatient only.
   2   Yes, as an outpatient only.
   3   Yes, as an inpatient and outpatient.

8. Total time spent in individual or group counseling:
   0   No previous care received.
   1   Less than one month.
   2   1–3 months.
   3   4–12 months.
   4   1–2 years.
   5   Over 2 years.

9. Who suggested you come to this office?
   0   Physician or psychiatrist.
   1   Friend or relative.
   2   Clergyman.
   3   Employer or school.
   4   Judge or attorney.
   5   Other _____

10. In the past year I have received medical treatment for:
    1. _____
    2. _____
    3. _____

11. I take the following prescription drugs (state dose and frequency):
    1. _____
    2. _____
    3. _____
    4. _____

12. Have you had a physical examination within the last month?
    0   No.
    1   Yes.
        By Dr. _____
        Address: _____
        _____

13. How many years of schooling have you completed?
    0   8 years or less.
    1   Some high school.
    2   Graduated from high school.
    3   Some college.
    4   Bachelor's Degree.
    5   Graduate school or other post college training.
    6   Graduate degrees(s)
        (Please list) _____
        _____

14. My income is:
    - 0   I have no income.
    - 1   from family or relatives.
    - 2   all or partly from welfare.
    - 3   largely self-earned.
    - 4   Other _____

15. In the past year or two my income has significantly
    - 0   not changed.
    - 1   increased.
    - 2   decreased.

16. Was this change expected?
    - 0   No
    - 1   Yes

17. Have you felt recently that your work, school, or other major endeavor is worthwhile?
    -    1)   completely
    -    2)   largely
    - c   3)   moderately
    - b   4)   slightly
    - a   5)   not at all

18. During the past three months, how often have you made an effort to understand the feelings and ideas of the people who are important to you, even when you disagreed with them?
    - a   1)   never
    - b   2)   rarely
    - c   3)   sometimes
    -    4)   usually
    -    5)   all the time

19. How often have you been trying your best in work, school, or other major endeavor recently?
        1) all the time
        2) usually
c   3) sometimes
b   4) rarely
a   5) never

20. During the past three months, how often have eating and weight control been a problem for you?
a   1) all the time
b   2) frequently
c   3) sometimes
        4) rarely
        5) never

21. During the past three months, how often have the activities you've done for recreation been competitive?
        1) never
        2) rarely
c   3) sometimes
b   4) usually
a   5) always

22. During the past three months, how often have you been able to express in words your feelings of love, sadness, and anger to those who are important to you:
a   1) never
b   2) rarely
c   3) sometimes
        4) usually
        5) regularly

23. During the past three months, how often have you allowed yourself to be treated with lack of consideration?
   - 1) never
   - 2) rarely
   - c   3) sometimes
   - b   4) often
   - a   5) all the time

24. During the past three months, how often have you taken time out to play?
   - a   1) never
   - b   2) rarely
   - c   3) occasionally
   - 4) frequently
   - 5) very frequently

25. How often recently have you been under the influence of alcohol or recreational drugs when you played?
   - a   1) always
   - b   2) usually
   - c   3) sometimes
   - 4) rarely
   - 5) never

26. How often do you exercise continuously for a minimum of twenty-five minutes or more?
   - a   1) never
   - b   2) rarely _____ once a week or less
   - c   3) sometimes _____ less than three times a week
   - 4) often _____ three to six times a week
   - c   5) always _____ every day

27. How satisfied are you with the appreciation you receive for your work or other major endeavor?
   - a   1) not at all
   - b   2) slightly
   - c   3) moderately
   - 4) largely
   - 5) completely

28. During the past few months, approximately how often have you gone out to do something you enjoy?
    1) at least once a week
    2) three times per month
c 3) twice a month
b 4) once a month
a 5) never or almost never

29. How often has controlling your drug intake been a problem during the past three months?
    1) never
c 2) rarely
c 3) sometimes
b 4) frequently
a 5) all the time

30. What has been your grade point average during the past six months of school?
    1) I have not been attending school
c 2) A-average
    3) B-average
c 4) C-average
b 5) D-average
a 6) Less than D-average

31. During the past few months, have you felt loved and appreciated by the people you care about?
a 1) no, not at all
b 2) only a little bit
c 3) by some, but not by others
    4) usually
    5) yes, all the time

32. In general, how satisfied have you been with your current work or other major endeavor?
a 1) not at all
b 2) only slightly
c 3) somewhat
    4) mostly
    5) very satisfied

33. How often have you been treating the important people in your life with respect and consideration recently?
    1) all the time
    2) usually
c 3) sometimes
b 4) rarely
a 5) never

34. Excluding vacation time, during the last two months, how often have you been absent from school or work?
    1) 0 days
    2) 1–3 days
c 3) 4–6 days
b 4) 7–9 days
a 5) over 10 days
    6) not applicable

35. On the average, how often have you felt well enough to do what you would like to do during the past three months?
    1) never
a 2) one day a week or less
b 3) two or three days a week
c 4) four to five days a week
    5) six days a week
    6) every day

36. On the average, how often have you had fun during the past three months?
    1) more than twice a week
    2) once or twice a week
c 3) several times a month
b 4) about once a month
a 5) never

37. During the past three months, how often have you received enough understanding, caring, and comforting?
  a   1) never
  b   2) rarely
  c   3) sometimes
       4) usually
       5) all the time

38. How often do you smoke cigarettes?
       1) never
       2) about 1 cigarette or less per day
  c   3) less than 1/2 pack per day
  b   4) 1/2 - 1 pack per day
  a   5) more than 1 pack per day

39. Do the people you care about readily accept your warmth,
understanding, and caring?
  a   1) no, never
  b   2) rarely
  c   3) some readily accept it, but others don't
       4) most of them do
       5) all of them do

40. How much stress have you had recently from external
sources (death of loved ones, illness, job problems,
divorce, etc.)?
       1) none
       2) very little
  c   3) some
  b   4) quite a bit
  a   5) a lot

41. How often recently have you been listening carefully and
offering comfort to the people who are important to you?
  a   1) never
  b   2) rarely
  c   3) sometimes
       4) usually
       5) all the time

42. How often have you felt good about yourself recently?
    1) all the time
    2) usually
   c 3) sometimes
   b 4) rarely
   a 5) never

43. On the average, how much alcohol (beer, wine or liquor) have you had during the past three months?
   a 1) more than three drinks a day
   b 2) three drinks a day
   c 3) one or two drinks a day
    4) less than one drink a day
    5) none

44. Has anyone (family, friends, people at work, police, etc.) expressed concern about your drinking during the past three months?
   a 1) yes, more than one person has
   b 2) only one person has
    3) no

45. During the past three months, on the average, how often have you taken marijuana?
    1) never
    2) once a week or less
   c 3) two to five times a week
   b 4) about once a day
   a 5) more than once a day

46. How often recently have you been getting enough relaxation time?
    1) every day
    2) almost every day
   c 3) three or four days a week
   b 4) one or two days a week
   a 5) less than once a week

47. On the average, during the past three months, how often have you taken LSD, PCP (angel dust), mescaline or any other hallucinogens?
    1) never
    b 2) less than once a month
    a 3) once a month or more

48. On the average, during the past three months, how often have you taken cocaine, diet pills, speed or other "uppers"?
    a 1) once a month or more
    b 2) less than once a month
    3) never

49. On the average, during the past three months, how often have you taken barbiturates, sleeping medications, tranquilizers (such as Valium, Xanax, Buspar) or other "downers"?
    1) never
    c 2) once a month or less
    b 3) two to three times a month
    b 4) about once a week
    a 5) more than once a week

50. Do you feel as if you're being challenged by something you've been doing recently and that you're growing as a result?
    1) completely
    2) largely
    c 3) moderately
    b 4) slightly
    a 5) not at all

51. During the past three months, on the average, how often have you had difficulty with your sleep habits?
    a 1) every night
    b 2) more than once a week
    c 3) once a week .
    4) less than once a week
    5) never

52. When you are upset, how often do you seek out, warmly accept and deeply feel caring or comforting from people you care about?
       1) all the time
       2) usually
  c 3) sometimes
  b 4) rarely
  a 5) never

53. How satisfied are you with the financial rewards you receive for your work?
  a 1) not at all
  b 2) slightly
  c 3) moderately
       4) largely
       5) completely

54. During the past three months, how often have you been satisfied with your sex life?
  a 1) not at all
  b 2) rarely
  c 3) sometimes
       4) usually
       5) always
       6) sex is not an issue for me at this time

55. Have you considered ending your own life during the past three months?
       1) no, never
  c 2) yes, less than once a week
  b 3) once or twice a week
  a 4) a few times a week
  a 5) daily or almost daily

56. Do any of your blood relatives have a history of suicide or serious depression?
  d 1) yes
       2) no
       3) I don't know

57. Do any of your blood relatives have a history of psychiatric illness requiring hospitalization?
   d 1) yes
       2) no
       3) I don't know

58. Do any of your blood relatives have a history of alcoholism or problem drinking?
   d 1) yes
       2) no
       3) I don't know

59. Do any of your blood relatives have a history of criminal activity?
   d 1) yes
       2) no
       3) I don't know

60. Have you been honest in answering these questions?
       1) yes
   b 2) mostly
   a 3) not really

Please note that some of the answers were prefixed by A, B, C or D.

In order to score yourself on this self-assessment questionnaire, please give yourself three points for each a, two points for each b and one point for each c and d. Total a, b and c will be weighted in this way:

Total a _____ multiply by 3 = _____
Total b _____ multiply by 2 = _____
Total c = _____
Total d = _____

Total score = _____

A, B, and C indicate how well you can take care of *you*. Each D indicates increased susceptibility to stress.

Your total score give you an idea of how well you're doing with your life.

TOTAL
SCORE   YOU ARE CARING FOR YOURSELF:

0–4 .... very well
5–9 .... reasonably well
10–19 .... not too well
20–29 .... poorly
30 or more .... self-destructively

Life is like that rather perverse game, golf. The higher the score the more you're slipping. In life you can never get your score to the "perfect" level. There's just too much unexpected change and stress. But what you can do is learn to minimize the impact of the "bad" changes, to read the telltale signs in your life and make it work for you.

I WISH YOU COURAGE IN THIS ENDEAVOR.

Thomas N. Rusk, M.D.

Copyright 1980
Revised 1991

CLIENT WORKSHEET

NAME _____ THERAPIST _____ DATE _____

MY MAJOR
PROBLEMS ARE   1. _____

                      2. _____

                      3. _____

                      4. _____

                      5. _____

NEEDS

A. I feel genuinely loved by someone other than my parents
   or my children:

   0___/___/___/___/___/___/___/___/___/___/
   not at all   very much

B. I feel in control of my life situation:

   0___/___/___/___/___/___/___/___/___/___/
   not at all   very much

C. I feel worthwhile:

   0___/___/___/___/___/___/___/___/___/___/
   not at all   very much

D. I have fun:

   0___/___/___/___/___/___/___/___/___/___/
   not at all   very much

GOALS

I would like to change my life by behaving differently in the following specific ways:

1. _____   4. _____

2. _____   5. _____

3. _____   6. _____

HOPE

I predict I will accomplish *my* goals listed above:

A. Totally   C. Partially
B. Mostly   D. Not at all

CONSULTATION AGREEMENT
PART 1
CONSULTANT

1. I agree to serve as your consultant to help you achieve mutually agreed upon goals which include:
   a) developing increased self-sufficiency and self-respect;
   b) avoiding permanent harm to you;
   c) relief from your symptoms;
   d) balancing your conflicting needs; and
   e) fostering your ability to heal yourself.

2. I see myself as a strong, confident, healthy, well-informed expert despite the errors I inevitably make.

3. Not being all knowing nor all powerful, I cannot guarantee results other than that you can increase your self-esteem just by having the courage to experiment with your life.

4. I will avoid using you to satisfy my needs except insofar as you can help me feel that I contribute by helping you and to the extent that you have agreed to reimburse me for my services.

5. I feel the responsibility of striving toward the ideal of providing my services as efficiently as possible, that is, the maximum service with the minimal possible expenditure of time and cost.

6. During the time we contract to spend together in our consultations, I will exclusively devote my interest and energy to you. In between those consultations, I will not be readily available as I will be attending to others, including myself. It's obvious but worth saying: I have the same responsibility for my life that you have for yours.

Signature of Consultant

Copyright 1980 T. N. Rusk, M.D.

CONSULTATION AGREEMENT
PART 2
CONSULTEE

1. I want to accept full responsibility for myself. I realize that my health largely depends on how I conduct my life—how I think, how I feel and what I do. I'm aware that blaming anything or anyone won't help me.

2. I came here to improve my life and that means I may need to change how I feel and think as well as how I treat myself. I am aware that as part of my changing, I may decide to change friends, job, spouse or lifestyle.

3. I know that anything less than my full participation will lead nowhere.

4. I am willing to enter into open, trusting communication and will consider your feedback in order to benefit my growth.

5. I understand that unrecognized thoughts, feelings and desires can profoundly influence my life and lead to or aggravate physical and emotional distress.

6. I understand I must experiment with different ways of thinking, feeling and behaving in order to find ways that suit me best. I know that no one way will work forever so I must learn to experiment while monitoring myself and my environment continuously to find the best way for me at any time. I realize that trying out new ways will at times feel awkward, artificial, and uncomfortable—even frightening at first.

7. I know you expect me to meet my financial obligations promptly and understand that I will pay for all time reserved unless cancelled 48 hours in advance.

I am consulting _____ to assist me in my efforts to change.

Please initial to indicate you understand. This does not necessarily imply your agreement.

Copyright 1979 T. N. Rusk, M.D.

258

TAPE RECORDING AGREEMENT

I strongly urge you to allow me to tape record our sessions so you may take the tapes home for your review. Clients originally suggested this approach. Many have reported great benefits well beyond simply refreshing their memories of the sessions. Maximal benefit comes from thorough review in the 24 hours following each session. Additional value comes from further review later.

Several cautions must be given:

1. Do not play these tapes for others or leave them where they can be found and played. They are for your exclusive and private use.

2. Although no lasting negative effects have occurred from others hearing these tapes, you must shoulder all the risks involved should anyone else do so with, or without, your permission. If you wish to gain the benefit of tape review without risking loss of confidentiality, simply listen to our session immediately afterwards and destroy the tape, or leave it at our office, after your review.

I understand the risks involved in tape recording our sessions.

_____   _____
Date   Client's signature

Permissions and Credits

Permission to reprint from the following book and periodicals is gratefully acknowledged:

Excerpts from *Love's Executioner* by Irvin D. Yalom. Copyright 1989 by Irvin D. Yalom. Reprinted by permission of Basic Books, a division of HarperCollins Publishers Inc.

The Harvard Medical School Mental Health Letter, Lester Grinspoon, M.D., Editor. 74 Fenwood Road, Boston, MA 02115. June 1990 (Vol. 6 No. 12) and December 1990 (Vol. 7 No. 6) issues.

Yoga Journal, Stephan Bodian, Editor. 2054 University Avenue, Berkeley, CA 94704. March/April 1991 issue.

Other briefly quoted sources include:

The MacMillan Dictionary of Quotations (New York: The MacMillan Publishing Company), 1987, 1989.

Creation Myths, Marie-Louise von Franz (Dallas: Spring Publications, Inc.), 1972.

Bioenergetics, Alexander Lowen, M.D. (New York: Viking Penguin), 1975.

Healing the Child Within, Charles L. Whitfield, M.D. (Deerfield Beach, FL: Health Communications, Inc.), 1987.

The Myth of Psychotherapy, Thomas Szasz (Syracuse University Press), 1978, 1988.

Children of Psychiatrists and Other Psychotherapists, Thomas Maeder (New York: Harper & Row). Copyright 1989 by Thomas Maeder.

Against Therapy, Jeffrey M. Masson (New York: Atheneum), 1988.

Psychoanalysis: The Impossible Profession, Janet Malcolm (New York: Random House), 1982.

The Seduction of Madness, Edward Podvoll (New York: HarperCollins), 1990.

The American Heritage Dictionary, Second College Edition (Boston: Houghton Mifflin), 1985.

State of the World 1991, Lester R. Brown (New York: W.W. Norton & Company), 1991.

A Course in Miracles (Glen Ellen, CA: Foundation for Inner Peace), 1976.

The Fifth Discipline, Peter M. Senge (New York: Doubleday), 1990.

Essentials of Business Ethics, Peter Madsen, Ph.D., and Jay M. Shafritz, Ph.D., Editors (New York: Penguin Books), 1990.

Intrapraneuring, Gifford M. Pinchot III (New York: Harpar & Row), 1985.